Square Jaw

and Big Heart

The life and times
of a Hollywood actor

D1737198

By Charles Napier
with Dante W. Renzulli, Jr.

Dedication

Charles Napier:
To my sons Whit and Hunter, my daughter Meghan
and to my friend and co-author Dante,
for making this book happen.

Dante W. Renzulli Jr.:
To my wife Pat, and children,
Joanne, Michelle, Bill and Liz.

Published in the USA by:
BearManor Media
P O Box 71426
Albany, Georgia 31708
www.bearmanormedia.com

ISBN 978-1-59393-624-2

Printed in the United States of America.

Book and cover design by Darlene Swanson of Van-garde Imagery, Inc.
Cover photo courtesy of The Russell A. Meyer Charitable Trust and Julio Dattavio, Photo Curator. See website: www.russmeyer.com

Contents

PR shot from the 1980's

Preface

Wherever I go, people will look at me as if they recognize me. They see that square jaw with the big smile. They may not know my name, but they know that face. That happens when you have been an actor for almost forty years, appearing in over 100 films and innumerable TV shows and commercials.

It has occurred to me that I have visited so many people in the privacy of their home via TV, that it's no wonder people (for the most part) treat me almost like family. I've been in their homes for so long that sometimes I feel like I am "the world's friend." I used to look at the TV antenna (remember them?) on top of a house and think, "I've been to your house."

Once while I was filming an obscure movie in the Northern Apennines region of Italy, I took a break and I wandered into some small remote village. Naturally I sought out the local bar for some nourishment. There was a black and white TV behind the bar, being watched by the local villagers. I took a seat at the bar. I look over at the TV. The *Dukes of Hazzard* was on, dubbed in Italian. Suddenly I appear on the screen, speaking perfect Italian. I had done a couple episodes of this show, but I did them in English.

The locals there started to do double takes, comparing the image on the TV with the American sitting at their village bar. I smiled at them, and they knowingly smiled back. Since I really didn't speak Italian, I offered a toast in English. I bought a round of drinks and we all became friends. Then I disappeared out the door, as if a ghost or phantom. I realized that my face is known all over, whether in some remote village of Italy or in the big cities of the United States. When you look at the sum of a man's life, there's something to be said for that.

I wrote this book to give you a perspective of what it is like to be an actor who makes his living in the movie and TV business. I may not be a major star, but I had enough talent to work for over forty years at it. I've known and worked with some of the great (and not so great) stars and talent of our times. I've loved it and I hope you enjoy my story.

— Charles Napier

Beginnings

Life began for me in Scottsville, Allen County, Kentucky on April 12, 1936. My father was a farmer and also a mail carrier. I had a younger brother and an older sister. Unfortunately we lost my brother, when I was very young.

I remember it was cold, very cold. The year was 1938 and I was two years old. How can anyone remember anything at that age? I did and still do. My dad broke the cold silence with these words, "Your brother is dead." Then he left. My sister started screaming. She was five and understood. My dead brother had a name, Thomas Franklin Napier. I can't recall the exact date but it is recorded somewhere.

This event took place in a rural area of Kentucky, Allen County. Scottsville was the county seat. I'm told we had 80 or so acres. Tobacco was our cash crop and was always sold just before Christmas time. The house was a one bedroom clapboard shack. An open fireplace and cook stove was our only heat. Light came from a coal oil (kerosene) lamp. I can still smell that acrid smell today. The road outside was gravel and if one looked left from the front porch, it led to the Methodist Church. This church was the hub and meeting place for several fanatical families, who gathered every boring Sunday AM to listen to some ignorant preacher rave and rant about sin, sin, sin. If being pure every day of the week wasn't enough, they held revivals every summer for two weeks. The point of this purgatory was the purification of the soul and "getting saved." "Getting saved" was never quite explained to me but I was filled to the max with guilt. It was a terrifying moment with the women sitting on one side, the men on the other side.

These women would leap straight up into the air shouting and babbling incoherently, speaking in tongues. They would advance toward the bad boys sitting in the back row. Most of them couldn't take the pressure and bolted for the door. Those unfortunate ones who were caught were literally dragged, kicking and screaming, to the altar, also called the "moaner's bench." There they were prayed over, prodded, and pounded into heaven's gate. One confession wasn't enough. Each year at revival, you were expected to fess up again and again. Once I learned to lie flat on the floor and pretend religious seizures, I realized it was a great position to look up the women's dresses. We had one preacher who had also discovered this little pleasure, and was usually the first one to hit the floor in a full frontal prone position.

My father was born in 1888; my mother in 1898. My Dad, Linus Pitts Napier, was 49 years old when I was born. LP (as he was called) was a small, no nonsense, serious man, who seldom smiled. He lived to be three months short of 104 years old. My father was born in Allen County, Kentucky. The Napiers can trace their heritage back to a Dr. Thomas Napier, who supposedly arrived from Scotland in the late 1800s. My mother was Sara Lena Loafman.

My mother was not from our community, and was naturally isolated from her side of the family. My father served as a medic during WWI and was wounded in the Argon Forest sometime in 1918. Returning home, he somehow met my mother, who lived in another county. Courting in those days was quite a challenge, as the major mode of transportation was a horse or mule back. Henry Ford had just begun to make inroads into this forgotten part of the world, but somehow Dad had acquired one and thus he brought home his bride. Both parents were of middle age when we kids were born, thus we had a dose of early 19th century attitudes, superimposed on our young, impressionable minds at a very tender age.

We had a farm of about 80 or so acres. The chief money crop was tobacco, which was sold around Christmas time each year. Money, real cash money, was hard to come by. No credit cards were used in those days; it was all cash. Food was raised on the farm. Only coffee and sugar were purchased. We had two horses, Bob and Betty, and a mule (his name escapes me). My greatest fear was being attacked each and every day by a rooster. It was called flogging. My dad beat the shit out of this evil bird but to no avail. I could shoot a 22 cal. rifle at the age of four and, as soon as opportunity presented itself, I drilled this bastard between the eyes. No small feat I assure you when being stalked. My first victory. This farm was eerie. Mamma always said when you heard a whippoorwill call after dark, someone was going to die. My cousin, Dr. Willard Blankenship (very talented and famous), told me that the Napiers married Browns. The reason? They were slavers. Not a very desirable past I can assure you, but I remember the old slave quarters at Aunt Johnnie's place. Still there today, I guess.

This part of Kentucky suffered the evils of the Civil War. Kentucky was a border state. Brother fought against brother. Father against son. Those hatreds exist even today. The mountain feuds were not necessarily about the Hatfields and McCoys, but about deep seated hatreds left over from that dark and evil conflict. Raiders on both sides struck deep into the heart of this state.

When I was about five, we moved. Gone were the cry of the whippoorwills. Gone were the woods that kept me frightened. Gone was the red clay earth I even used to eat. I was about to enter a new world.

My mother's aunt was called Aunt Pearl. She was married to a cultured gentleman (a preacher) we called Uncle Potter. Aunt Pearl had class. Even then, not even knowing what class was, I could recall. All socializing was done at church. Everyone's life revolved around that church and the harsh rules and regulations governing our every move. Every thought was scrutinized by these bucolic people.

I recall being placed in Uncle Potter's car. For some reason I was fascinated by the hood ornament. As if in a dream, we rode for what seemed like an eternity, and finally came to a stop at a little house on what was called the Glasgow Pike. I was stunned! There were houses on both sides of our little place. Strange people lived across the road (not really a street but a two lane highway) and lots of cars passed, much to my amazement.

It was here that I was introduced to bullies, sex, and fights. It all started first at Scottsville Elementary School. It was some three or four miles away, in Scottsville. I remember the first day. My dad had gotten a job as a rural mail carrier. Boy he was pleased. A steady weekly check. He was a very frugal man. Believe it or not, in the 1930's, he had purchased a 100 acre farm for less than 5000 dollars. And he held on to that farm. We also owned the little house on Glasgow Pike. I still have some memories of it. A family across the road had ten or twelve kids. No one supervised anyone in those days. You simply went out on your own and got the shit beat out of you for starters. When I inquired why this happened, I was told by the older brother to pick out one of his brothers who was younger, and smaller than me, and apply an ass whipping on him. I did so, but soon found myself feeling like a bully, so I stopped. In keeping with their simple and primitive ways, I was introduced to sex with the sisters of this family.

World War II

World War II was in full bloom. Some of the older boys and all of my first cousins were fighting somewhere. Duffle bags stuffed with German paraphernalia began arriving at the home of our family. Lugers, German helmets, flags, daggers. I can still smell the leather from the belts. The smell was of Nazi Germany. A smell I could still identify today. One could almost sense the evil that had come upon the world. We gathered scrap iron for the war effort. Gasoline was rationed, but actually we kids never paid much attention to that stuff. We were too busy playing, building homemade cars. The wheels were made from sawed off tree trunks. Power was supplied by the bigger boys. I was picked as one of the drivers because of my size. On Saturdays, some of us walked the three or four miles to Scottsville and attended the Lyric Theatre. There, we were exposed to Hopalong Cassidy, Red Rider, Lash Larue, and Bobby Blake as Little Beaver (much later, I would share the screen with Bobby in the TV show *Baretta*).

We played in an old barn. There we built a phony bar, complete with whiskey bottles we garnered from the ditches leading from town to our neighborhood. It was strange that Allen County, classified as "dry" (no booze was legally sold) had so many closet drunks. However, this didn't register at the time. So we played bad guys against the good guys. No acting lessons required. I've often said, when asked about the acting profession, that you need no license, no education. All an adult has to do is drop back into an infantile level, and be the character. We didn't go off and think about motivation. Really, I think it's that way the world over.

One day, we heard the rumble of strange traffic sounds, and were stunned when an endless procession of every type of army vehicle crept down this two lane road. Eventually this convoy stopped and soldiers began digging foxholes, setting up tents and manning machine guns. Man, this was great! Real soldiers. They were part of the 101 Airborne Division, the "Screaming Eagles" who would, within a few short months, be taking an ass kicking at Bastogne and other bloody battlegrounds in Europe.

Like lonely soldiers almost everywhere, they liked kids. I carried water for them for five cents a bucket. They let us play with their machine guns. They also conned us out of lots of German Waffen SS lugers and other paraphernalia. Very soon, they wouldn't need these spoils of war, as they were to receive their own baptism of fire.

On December 7, 1941, my father came home from work in his 1941 Ford. Being a federal employee, he had gas and a new car to carry the mail. I sensed something unusual about the way he ground to a halt. I'll never forget the look on his face. Being a WWI vet and having ten or twelve nephews acting as bomber pilots to grunt infantrymen engaged in combat every single day, he had a reason to be concerned. "The Japs have bombed Pearl Harbor," he growled. I didn't know what a Jap was. Where the hell was Pearl Harbor? What news we kids got was over the radio, movie theatre war reels or the party line telephone. We had a radio of some kind that would bring in far away stations. One night we heard the terrified voice of a captured American soldier crying out from somewhere in Europe. My father copied down his name and address and wrote to his parents. Sounds silly and primitive? I come from a different time warp and place, my friends. These soldiers were gone for four or five years. The only communication they had with loved ones was an occasional censored letter (that's right, *censored*).

A gold star in the window of a little shack meant they had someone fighting in the terrible war. I can't remember what was displayed when that soldier was killed, but there was a symbol. My cousin, Jesse Lee Woodward, was General Patton's driver. Corbin Napier was up to his ass in "krauts." Hating Germans and Japs was the order of the day. Another cousin (my favorite) was John G. Napier. He flew B24s and other types of bombers. He went from lieutenant to lieutenant colonel in a few short months, as planes were shot out of the skies. I recall he came home on leave early in the war and buzzed the town of Scottsville at tree top level in a B24 bomber. He later was a wing commander at Langly AFB in Virginia. My God, he looked like a hero, with a beautiful wife named Juanita.

April 12, 1945 was my birthday. President Roosevelt also died that day. Like him or hate him, he put a face on the war. Then there was this little guy, with the glasses and funny looking suit. This ex-haberdasher from Missouri. Harry Truman was suspect from the beginning, but soon shook off this innocent image by dropping Little Man and Fat Boy on Hiroshima and Nagasaki. So what, they were Japs.

We in Kentucky had never seen a person of Japanese heritage. All we knew was that the war was now over. WWII was simple in definition. Good defeating bad. Right against wrong. Hitler and Tojo were the people to hate. The people went mad with joy all over America. It was actually over.

I reached the age of sixteen. That magical number! For boys, that means cars, cars and more cars. And a full thatch of pubic hair. Of course, in 1952, no one 16 years of age had one of these dream machines, with the exception of a couple rich kids. They were all hated, but never turned down. We would pile in the back seat, circle the court house square on Saturday Nights and then hit the 101, double lane highway in a death defying race with the other rich kid and his thrill-seeking passengers. Those of us who didn't have access to such a dream machine begged and pleaded for use of the family church car … in my case, this was a 1950 two-door Ford. My father always had enough money somehow to own a decent automobile. In fact, his job as a rural mail carrier allowed him to eventually own a new Jeep which made it possible to navigate his route of perhaps twenty or thirty miles of dirt roads, five days a week.

After much pleading I was allowed to drive that Ford. Very quickly, I began to remake this beast into an image I could be rather proud of. Notwithstanding the fact that everyone "knew" it was still the family church car, I soon began to transform this machine into what would be considered today, a rolling piece of white trash junk. First, the tires were given a very cheap version of whitewalls. Then came the balloon headers, mail ordered straight from some magazine. Imagine the thrill of hearing that roar! Everyone inside Carvers

Cafe looked on in awe. I got rubber in the first two gears. Side mirrors were accepted. Mud flaps were totally taboo, except for the occasional cloddish farm boy who dared venture into town. Getting specific contempt was this goofy looking guy called "Short Wave Hicks," so named for the twenty or so antennas sprouting from his old jalopy. In fact he had no radio of any sort, much less short wave. CB radio was years in the future.

Charles Napier (2008).
From the author's collection.

Scottsville, Kentucky

Scottsville, Kentucky was the birthplace of the Dollar General Corporation. Cal Turner Sr., who I knew as Old Man Turner, and his father would turn their little dry goods store on the square into a Dollar General empire. From that one store, there are now 8,000 stores all over the country. I knew this family well, very well. Cal's daughter, Laura Jo Turner, was my girlfriend from the 6th grade through high school. At the time, Mr. Turner, with his son, Cal Jr. and Laura Jo, lived in a small house on Main Street. Laura Jo (southern girls always seem to have two names) and I did some serious courting in that living room.

Let me try and set the perimeters of Scottsville, in the early 1950's. The old courthouse in Scottsville was the heart of the town. Set on its highest point was the emblem of an eagle, peppered with bullet holes. This was the result of hoards of drunks celebrating the end of WWII in 1945. Never again would I see such a pouring out of tension and relief. This had been a war of right and wrong. Many all over the world had paid the ultimate price. God help those who had been labeled a draft dodger. As I recall, what few had the bad fortune to bear this distinction were run out of town, or ostracized the rest of their lives.

In front of this splendid old court house, one could see an occasional bootlegger dragged in and thrust upon the hard asphalt. The contents of this ill profession would be poured down the drain, except what was confiscated as "evidence" by the sheriff and judge. Votes were bought for a dollar or a half pint of "Jim Beam." Then there was the stockyard. The magical voice of the auctioneer mixed with the bawling and mooing of cattle, the baas of sheep and goats, and the screams of pigs being pole axed. The acrid smells of animal shit seemed to act as an elixir. Outside the selling pens, one stood enthralled, watching the medicine man turn a suspicious bottle of piss from amber to clear in about five seconds. It worked! Grown men were fighting over this magical liquid: To have your urine be clear made perfect sense at that time. See, clear days were better than cloudy. Later on when we started wearing underwear, it made perfect sense. No embarrassing stains for suspicious mothers checking out such items with an evil eye.

Alcohol wasn't much of a temptation until one turned 18 and graduated from high school. No one wondered why. There were no tempting drugs, except the girls. The girls! They were pretty much divided into "good and bad." The general consensus of opinion among the boys came down to this. There were too damn many "good girls" and not enough "bad." I shall say no more about the "good girls" but heap praise on the occasional "bad one." A particular favorite had the unique nickname of "Mundo."

One could hear the lusty call of "Did you get any of that blue liquid Mundo?" As I recall, blue liquid Mundo was a detergent of some kind. What this girl had to do with a detergent, I shall never know and never asked. But she sure as hell turned my generation into a unique bonding group. Talking about this lurid side of life now is a little embarrassing, but back then "getting laid" was considered a serious life experience bordering on the very meaning of life. One had a better change getting struck by lightning than stumbling across such a treasure as Mundo. Chivalry wasn't practiced much, except opening the car door for the "good girls." In dealing with Miss Mundo. a car packed with horny teenagers simply pulled up in front of the shack called home. Opened the trunk, honked the horn and Mundo would come galloping down the hill, leap into the trunk and off we would go. Rocks would be flying as we sped away with our treasure. Sex was, is now, and always will be the driving force of mankind. At least that's been my observation.

Sunset Springs was a diner with a dance floor, a few miles out of town. It was our gathering spot. After lurking outside the Methodist Church in downtown Scottsville for what seemed an eternity, the "good girls" would come running out, hop into these redneck chariots we called cars. Off we go to Sunset Springs Diner. Serious speeds and races somehow got us there at 90 mph on bald tires. We drank Cokes, gossiped, fell in love, fought over women and did all the other things kids did in those days. Even Elvis wasn't around. TV was an event that caused people to gather in a backwater place called "Bunkum." We sat on boards, atop nail kegs and watched wrestling on a TV set. About 10pm or so on Sunday Night, after leaving Sunset Springs, one would go "park" with his "steady." After a half hour of bumping and grinding, the "steady" was dropped off and the "boys" all headed to Carver's cafe for gossip and greasy cheeseburgers from the dirty hands of Ralph Carver. It was no little secret that Ralph also sold "rubbers." Everyone bought one at least every other month. One had to keep up a front. I would imagine there is a holy grail of condoms outside Carver's cafe to this day.

I was sixteen. My buddies were Tommy, Jimmy and Mutt. We were inseparable. Jimmy had an old car called "scooter." The top had been cut off affording plenty of fresh air and sunshine. When it rained, that was tough shit. One of our friends, named Billy, had been killed that year in a tractor accident. I shall never forget the grief of his mother and father having to bury their only son. Children, looking back, seemed more important in the material sense. They were workers. In my case, that was hard to enforce since I could run faster than my father. Billy's father and mother sort of took us three boys into their lives. We all had relatively unstable relations with parents, if we had parents. Mr. Woods let us build a cabin on Barren River. This was an idyllic time to be growing up and I honestly think we realized that. We fished, swam, watched out for the feds for a couple of old guys who had a still, making moonshine. We all experienced our first hangover at that cabin in the summer of 1952. After partaking of some of old John's rotgun moonshine whiskey, we awoke at dawn in a pile of puke, sadder but not much wiser. The feeling was beyond sick. It was as if someone had run a battery brush up your ass and you had to ask if you were still alive and the only feelings were hot and cold.

This little vacation came to a screeching halt before summer was over. I was given a job at the Douglas food store. Of course, I was turned into a mule, lugging heavy sacks of coffee and sugar up the stairs from an evil smelling hole in the ground called "the basement." It was here I developed a taste for salami and bologna, filched of course from the meat counter. Mr. Douglas decided he was much better off not having me scarfing his meats, so I was "dismissed." My father never got over this humiliation. He kept bringing it up to me until he died at l04. My fortunes were destined to be changed for the better that year.

A wealthy man named Mr. Reed always seemed to notice me. Not in a sexual way, but in the way older men looked upon younger boys they wanted to help mold into hard working honest citizens. To my astonishment, he offered me a chance to be his chauffeur. He always called me "Cotton," because of my blond hair, I guess. This opportunity to get paid to drive a car was beyond belief. He bought me decent clothes and we set off in a Lincoln limo for the big city of Louisville, where he had a soft drink plant.

A dream had come true for a country boy. At age l6, I was driving Mr. Read around. Not just around, we're talking Louisville, Kentucky in the l950's. The famous Brown Hotel, where we often stayed, was more or less our home base when in Louisville. One morning we were having breakfast in the hotel. Mr. Read, always curious, motioned with his eyes toward a small, bald, fat man sitting at the counter. "That's Mr. Brown, the hotel owner," he mumbled. At the time I couldn't have cared less about Mr. Brown, yet something told me we were running with a different crowd than I had been brought up with.

Back to Louisville and the "boat." Her hull was constructed from steel at a boat yard on the Ohio River. Mr. Read designed her. She was christened "Friendship IV." It was about l2 feet wide and maybe 35 or 40 long. She was powered by two gas engines. You have to remember this was a "yacht" in the early fifties. Building it went quite fast. The day finally came where we had the hull hauled from Louisville to Lake Cumberland. As I recall, this convoy consisted of Kentucky State Police and several other assist vehicles. Some telephone or electric had to taken down along the way. People, along the way were upset. The roads back then were two lane; no four-lane super-slabs back then. The journey was probably less than a hundred miles and was no small feat.

Mr. Read and I were waiting in a small cafe at the lake when this convoy snaked its way down the hill to the shimmering waters of Lake Cumberland and Lee's boat dock. This was the home port for "Friendship IV." The vessel would be completed afloat. It would have a kitchen, bedrooms, even a grand piano. The boat could be steered from inside the pilot house or outside on deck. Seems Mr. Read had learned from the last three "holes," where people throw money, and thought of everything. At the age of 16 or 17, I became the Captain, general flunky, bartender and swabbie. We had a cook named Bush. Bush was African American, and he also hailed from Scottsville. Bush was terrified of water, so I blindfolded him until he was safely inside the boat and couldn't see the water.

My cousin, Aubrey Woodward, and his brother-in-law, Raymond Meador, and myself were the carpenters and cabinetmakers. When finished, this floating palace was a marvel to behold. Many of Mr. Read's business partners were wined and dined on this craft. Mr. Read had a nasty temper (most rich men do) and could be very intimidating. His vocabulary was rife with the best curse words. Somehow coming from him, these verbal attacks seemed appropriate and I soon learned to accept them. His patience reached a boiling point for me the day I was trucking expensive windows from Louisville to Lake Cumberland, which was about ten miles from Louisville. Some very expensive windows came loose from their moorings and crashed from the truck. I pulled over and stopped. There was broken glass everywhere.

I finally got the courage to report this disaster to Mr. Read, a major undertaking in those days. The phone system was like two Dixie Cups on a string. I took the cursing for a few minutes, then I screwed up some courage, and told him to go f*** himself and stick the friendship up his ass. I started hitch hiking back to what was called home. I wasn't on the road with my thumb out over thirty minutes when a car pulled up. Man gets out and says Mr. Read is sorry, and says he thinks of you as a son. I took this all in, pocketed the "grease" money, and said "Ok." I got back in the truck and headed back for another load. Mr. Read never mentioned it again.

Army Life

In 1954, I graduated from high school. My hopes for going to college were crushed when I went out for the basketball team at Middle Tennessee Tech, and I didn't make it. No scholarship. No money. No college. I talked to my Dad. He never gave much advice in life, but this time he told me to enlist in one of the armed services, and "find out what life is really about."

A couple of my close friends were also going in the armed services: Jim Wilson, Tommy Long, and Carlston Purdue. Wilson and I decided to flip a coin. Heads; we're heading to the Marines. Tails; we're going to the Army Airborne. It came up tails, so we enlisted with the Army under the "buddy" system. We just missed the Korean War.

After eight weeks training at Fort Knox, I was shipped to Fort Jackson. I volunteered for the Army Airborne, and I was attached to the 11th Airborne Division and stationed in Germany for three years.

When I got out of the service, I was now eligible to go to college under the GI Bill. I enrolled at Western Kentucky. My four years at WK were four of the best years of my life. After three years of having my life dictated to me in the Army, I was going to school and young girls were all around me. It was a great time, but I also developed social skills there, that I didn't have before. Those skills have helped me throughout my life.

My Acting Life Starts

Igraduated from Western Kentucky in 1961, with a B.S. degree as an art major. I returned to Allen County High as an assistant basketball coach and teacher. I took the place of an assistant coach, who went to Vietnam in the Army. Unfortunately I lost my job when he came back. Good for him; bad for me.

A friend of mine, Bill Hancock, suggested I try out for a play at Western Kentucky. I spoke with Dr. Russell Miller, who was head of the Western Kentucky drama department. He was aware of my college hijinks but nevertheless he agreed to have me join in his theatre group. So during the summer of 1963, I was in my first play, *Love Among the Ruins*. Later I was Iago in *Othello*, at the Alley Playhouse, also in Kentucky. Many years later I found out that a teenage John Carpenter (later a famous director) was in the audience while I played Iago. Seems his father was a music teacher at Western Kentucky and lived at the University.

I still needed a paying job, so when I got a job offer to teach art in Florida, I took off. I got a one-room apartment at the Francis Wilson Playhouse in Clearwater, Florida. I taught at the Kennedy Middle School, also in Clearwater. During my time off from teaching, I started to do plays at the Playhouse, including *Becket*.

I had an interesting encounter during that play. I was in the middle of the prayer speech, playing Beckett. Perino Mascerino was playing King Henry. In character, I am required to come off the stage, and kneel at an altar next to the audience. I was praying my ass off when I glanced up. I was looking into the most piercing and terrifying blue eyes I have ever seen, before or since. I immediately lost my contact with the Holy Spirit, and was terribly distracted. I fumbled trough the rest of the prayer and beat a hasty retreat to the safety of the stage.

Mercifully the play finally ended. When I took my curtain call, I looked for the woman with those eyes. Gone like the mist. Later backstage, as I changed to my civies, there was a knock on the dressing room door. I was handed a note, which said, "Bravo! You are invited to lunch. Olga Petrova." Petrova had just broken into my playing field. The "blue eyes" belonged to her.

She was in her 70's. She was great silent film star for Metro, born in Poland. As I got to know Olga, I was fascinated by her and her stories of old Hollywood. Among her lovers was Charlie Chaplin. She once told me, "Dear boy, life is truly a play. I perform every day. I dress to perform every day." She was aware of my growing ambition to make a living as an actor.

Fortuitously an event occurred that changed everything. I was involved in a bad head-on auto collision. The other driver came into my lane. There was a violent collision. I ended up with ninety stiches on the side of my face and a lot of bruises. As a result of the insurance settlement, I netted $6,000.

Now having the necessary funds, I spoke with Olga about going to New York to pursue my acting career. She told me, "Go my child." With the insurance money in my pocket, I took off for New York.

New York

I arrived in New York with a lot of dreams. I didn't get a job as an actor but I did get job at NBC, at Rockefeller Plaza. I was hired as a typist. From the time I was in school and then in the Army, I could type. I had this hope that I would meet the President of NBC, Julian Goodman. He was from the same area of Kentucky as me. I thought once I told him where I was from, he would help me get a job in TV or the movies. Never happened.

Although I went to a lot of casting calls, nothing came of it. I saw an ad in a New York paper for a role in *Othello*, in San Diego, California. I bought an old VW, and it was "California, here I come!"

San Diego

I arrived in San Diego and went to the Old Globe Theatre. I auditioned and I ended up working the entire theatrical season. We did *Othello*, *Twelfth Night*, among others. Tyrone Guthrie, a great stage actor, had said, "Once you taste the wine of the theatre, no other wine would do." The resident director, Edward Pason Call, encouraged me to be a stage actor. But my dreams and ambitions were to be in the movies, so I took off for LA.

Los Angeles

When I got to L.A., I had to eat, so I applied for a job as a substitute teacher. With my degree from Western Kentucky, I got the job at $80 per day. I could eat at least, but I still looked for jobs as an actor.

I would hang out at the Raincheck Room, a bar-restaurant on

Santa Monica Boulevard, where a lot of young actors congregated. There I met Dennis Hopper, Jack Nicholson, Peter Fonda, Harry Dean Stanton, and Anthony James. Stanton and I hit it off well, because we both were from the same area of Kentucky. These were pre-*Easy Rider* days, so a lot of these guys were not stars yet. They all got work in films, except me. I was always complaining to them about not getting acting jobs.

Jack Nicholson told me that they have to find me an agent, and then I'll get acting jobs. One night, an agent, Thelma White, comes into the restaurant with her dog. Jack knows her and drags me over to meet her. He tells her that I need an agent and asks her to talk to me. She agrees and I sit at her table. We talk. She gets up to leave, and as she waits for her car, the dog takes a dump. I clean it up. She tells me, "I guess I'll have to take you on now." Finally I had an agent thanks to Jack and a dog.

The first film I did was a Western. It was called *The Hanging of Jake Ellis*. It was an independent film, funded by a woman named Elisa Singman. Its budget was $37,000, and it was a pathetic soft core movie. Today it would be rated R, but then it was scandalous because it showed a woman's boobs. I made three films for Elsa, none of which were any good.

In order to get into the studios, I needed a union card. I had met Howard Rayfield, who was an executive with Paramount. He said he would help me get the card. He got me a bit part on *Mission: Impossible*, on TV. It was 1968 and I had my union card. The episode was titled "The Play." I actually had my first line on this show. I played a military guard, who patrolled the outside of a building with a German shepherd at his side. I told some scared delivery persons, "He only bites when I smile." There it was for the whole world to hear. *Charles Napier speaks on network TV.* The door was now open. I got an uncredited role on another TV show, *Hogan's Heroes,* and I had a line on that show too. Around this time, I also did a very lucrative commercial for Lucite Paints.

A picture from the set of the TV show, the original *Star Trek* (1969).
From the author's collection.

Star Trek

In 1969, there was an open audition at Paramount for a part in an episode of *Star Trek*, the original TV show. The part called for a hippy singer, who was also a song writer. I had no agent, no guitar, no music writing skills, and I wasn't a hippy. But I wanted that part because it was a substantial role and I would get a credit. In other words, I actually would get listed as an actor at the end of the show. *Very* important for a young actor.

I went to Sears and bought a guitar. A musician once told me that Johnny Cash only knew three chords. What was good enough for Johnny was good enough for me. I promptly learned three chords to get ready for my "big break." I showed up at the audition with my guitar, open neck shirt, fake gold chains, a red handkerchief wrapped around my brow, looking deranged. 200 other actors showed up too.

The wait was endless. Everyone was plunking, and preening for hours. But, after a while, boredom and frustration set in. Finally I was led by a very pissed off 3rd or 4th assistant director into a room (all assistant directors are pissed; they're *born* pissed). There were several exhausted people in the room, including the director, David Alexander.

For some insane reason, I leaped onto the coffee table in front these people. I roared out my version of "House of the Rising Sun," the only song I could play on the guitar. I was so into the music I didn't hear the orders to stop. Finally someone yanked on my bell bottoms and yelled "Fuckin' stop, you hippie drug addict. You got the part."

I had been hired on the spot. That was the only time that ever happened in my career. The only problem was that I lied a little. When I was asked, I told them I had a band and I could write music. Both of those statements were total bullshit. But I didn't care. I got the job. Every actor lies. If he doesn't, he dies. They call it "spin" today. The important thing is that I got my foot in the door. I would deal with the deceptions later.

Arthur Hyndiman, a writer on the show, gave me some song lyrics, and told me to come back the next day with "my band" and some music based on his lyrics. I went out to Hollywood Boulevard to look for a band. I ran into Deborah Downey, an actress, who I knew from the Elsa Singman movies. Her boyfriend was a musician. He agreed to help me get a band and write the music, but on one condition. I had to get Deborah a part in a *Star Trek* episode.

I show up the next day and I meet with the music conductor. I was supposed to pre-record the songs. After some discussion about music, he sizes me up and says: "You lied, didn't you? You can't write music." I admitted it. His reaction surprised me. He said, "I love it. I love putting something over on them (the producers)." We worked together to create six or seven songs.

I appeared on the show as Adam. I was dressed in a costume that made me look like "Barbarella." I looked ridiculous. The producer said I looked like an ugly chicken and he didn't like it, but there was no time to change. So I appeared on *Star Trek* looking like a deranged bird and sang my songs. The episode is called "The Way to Eden," and still appears on TV. I was a futuristic hippie flower child that somehow got on the Enterprise.

To this day I still get requests to appear at *Star Trek* fan conventions, because of that appearance back in 1969.

During this time period, I didn't get enough work as an actor to make a living. But I had a college degree, so I also worked as a substitute teacher. As a further backup, I worked as a valet, parking cars at a restaurant. I was doing all right now, and the restaurant valet job got me free food, which was good for my financial and physical health.

Moonfire

My next project was a film called *Moonfire*. This was an independent film developed by the writer, Michael Parkhurst. No one, including Michael, had the remotest idea what *Moonfire* was about or what it meant. The word sounded cool, so he used it. Basically it was about truck drivers. Some drivers claimed it meant the flames shooting from the twin stacks of their Peterbilt on a moonless night. Others said it was an experience one had to experience to know what it was. Did that make sense? I didn't think so.

On this movie I met an actor who became a good friend. The star of the movie was Richard Egan. He was in his 50s by then. He had been a major star with 20th Century Fox. He was a real gentleman but he could be tough when he wanted to be. Charles Durning (a great actor and friend) once told me a story about Richard. Egan was making a cowboy movie with Charles Bronson. Bronson was spitting tobacco juice into a fire that had been set up. Richard asked Bronson, "Would you stop spitting into the fire; it's very crude." Bronson reached down to his leg. Richard thought he was trying to get a knife. Richard didn't wait to find out, and he decked Bronson.

We were shooting in Arizona and it was late November. We had a break for Thanksgiving. Not having a lot of money, I was just going to stay in Arizona. Richard came over to me and told me his family was having a Thanksgiving dinner back in Beverly Hills. Feeling sorry for me, he asked me to return to LA with him and I agreed.

When we get to his house, I met his wife, actress Patricia Hardy. But his guests at dinner blew me away. There was Robert Mitchum, Rory Calhoun, and 12 priests (one of which was Richard's brother). Mitchum became a lifelong friend, with whom I later did some film work.

Another personality I got to know in this movie was Sonny Liston, the fighter. Sonny was a very imposing figure. At this point he was no longer fighting, having lost his heavyweight championship title to Cassius Clay (Mohammad Ali) in 1964. When I met him, he was hired as an actor in this movie. Most people remember him for his scowl, but in reality he was a friendly guy and a real practical joker.

Believe it or not, he couldn't read or write. He would sit in the lobby of the hotel pretending he was reading the newspaper. As for his acting, someone would have to read his lines to him and he would memorize them. Because of that fact, he didn't like it if they wanted to change his lines. He was a good man. I enjoyed his company. He was my friend until he died.

Overdrive Magazine

The writer-producer of *Moonfire*, Michael Parkhurst, had founded a magazine that was the only magazine for truckers, called *Overdrive*. Having been a long haul trucker himself, he saw an opportunity for publishing a magazine for the thousands of truckers in the nation. It was a very successful magazine. Except for Russ Meyer, the director-producer, Mike was the most eccentric man I have ever known.

In 1972, I approached Mike about something I could do while waiting for acting jobs. I pointed out to him that the magazine had no "on the road" reporter. I volunteered and he accepted. I hit the road with my VW mini bus, repainted with the word "Overdrive" emblazoned across each side. Armed with a typewriter and a camera, I was free to roam the nation's highways to look for stories.

One of my first assignments was to interview Evel Knievel, the infamous daredevil who crashed his motorcycle all over the US landscape. I found him in some cheap motel on Sunset Boulevard in L.A. The interview wasn't very memorable. The thing I do remember the way he handled his broken body, as he lurched around the room. He went to great lengths to explain each and every bone that had been broken or shattered. After awhile, we went out drinking. I don't recall anyone paying any attention to him, which surprised me since he was quite famous.

When we got back to the motel, we saw a bunch of teenagers hanging out. He was driving a specially made Cadillac station wagon, which he claimed was the only one ever built. The kids didn't know who he was, but they loved that car. Either to impress me or as an act of total impulsiveness, he tossed the keys to the kids and told them to take the car for a drive. Without another word he turned and limped through the motel lobby.

The writing-photographer job for *Overdrive* magazine started to take on a life of its own. The highpoint came in the truck strike of 1973. I had become the eyes and ears of the nation's truck drivers. Hunter Thompson of *Rolling Stone* and Ken Huff of *Time* magazine sought me out for the driver's perspective. Whether it's lettuce from Salinas, oranges from Florida, coal from Kentucky, steers from Texas, it has to travel by truck sometime. They were the last American cowboys. It was a heady time for me, as I was the voice of thousands of truckers.

This was the period that Citizens Band (CB) radios became all the rage and a method of instant communications between the truckers, sort of the e-mail of the road. "Handles" such as Thunder Chicken, Destroyer Escort, Frito Bandito, The Big Orange were used. The king of them all was Rice Paddy Daddy. He packed 5000 watts of punishing power. When he picked up the mike with that famous voice, and said "Breaker 19," a hushed and reverent silence fell on CB radio land. "That's a 10-4."

Alfred Hitchcock

Cut to 1973. Hollywood Boulevard. I was on my ass, living in a truck with a camper shell, which was parked on a lot owned by Russ Meyer, the producer. Never mind that he was a friend and a millionaire. Out of the generosity of his cheap heart, Russ allowed me to use the lot, without being harassed by the cops. At 37, I was living in a world of bashed and broken dreams.

One fine day, I was sitting on the curb of the Boulevard with a bunch of bums, drunks, and assorted scum, etc. Up pulls a black limousine. Out steps a man in a dark suit, who then orders the limo driver to quiz us bums. He walked around asking "Who or where is Charles Napier?"

I answered the call, and got in the limo. I sat on the calfskin seat, next to the man in the suit. I decided to remain quiet, while I got a drink of liquor from the well-stocked supply.

I had hardly taken a sip when we entered the pearly gates of Universal Studios. I had been there many times before. We approached a building with the famous profile of Alfred Hitchcock painted on it. As I finished my drink, the driver opened the door. The "suit" spoke to me: "Don't say a word; just do as I tell you."

I entered the building. A nervous secretary buzzed us inside to the celestial chambers of Alfred Hitchcock. I'll never forget the moment. About ten feet away. He was sitting in a chair with his back to me. It seemed I waited an eternal, theatrical time.

Dramatically Hitchcock turned the chair around and I was facing him, one of the most famous directors in movie history. Yet his eyes stayed on the "suit." As if in an echo chamber, I hear him say to the suit, "Tell him to turn around." The suit, sweating with fear, commands me, "Turn around." Transfixed, I obey.

Hitchcock then says, "Sign him." The suit says, "Yes sir." As we go out, the suit is pissed, but he says to me, "Look buddy, I don't know who you are or whatever, but you're one lucky guy because he just signed you to a contract, a yearly contract." My thoughtful reply: "Okay." Normally you have to beg for roles, now I would be ordered to do roles. I needed money. I had none. The suit tells me to go to the payroll office. I asked him what the pay was. He says, "I think it's $3500 a week." My wide-eyed response was, "You're kidding me." The annoyed suit says, "No, I'm not kidding. You will report Monday to the *Baretta* set." After *Baretta*, I did *Kojak, Rockford Files*, wherever they sent me.

Although Hitchcock signed me to a contract, my services were actually assigned to Universal Studios. From being homeless, my world changed radically in a matter of hours. Over the next few years, I appeared in many Universal TV shows. Ironically, I never worked a day in any movies or television shows directed by or connected to Hitchcock, nor did I ever see him again. Still the man radically changed my life.

Russ Meyer

Another man who had a big effect on my early movie career was director, producer, and writer, Russ Meyer. In the 1960s, he was derisively regarded as a schlock artist, who made skin flicks. Today, there are film festivals which celebrate his "artistry."

Russ was a combat photographer in Europe during WWII. He filmed both General Omar Bradley's First Army and General George Patton's Third Army. His combat footage was highly praised. One time I was with him on a plane, flying to London. He was reading a book about WWII. Suddenly he slammed the book closed, and muttered, "I'm probably the only guy alive who hated to see the War end." He considered his unit of combat photographers the only family he ever had. After the War, he would pay their way for their annual reunions.

When he came back from the War, he became a freelance photographer. He first started to take still shots for "nudie" magazines, including *Playboy*. He then started to make skin flicks. He hit the jackpot with a film called *The Immoral Mr. Teas*. It was the first soft core movie to make a lot of money. It made more than $1,000,000. As he continued to make these movies, he became a millionaire. Keep in mind, while these films were considered scandalous at the time, today these films would be rated R.

The first movie I made with him was *Cherry, Harry and Raquel* (1969). Working a Meyer movie was different from working in any other movie. He liked to shoot in the desert. Not only was the desert free, but the cast couldn't escape. Russ liked the juxtaposition of the beautiful girls with the harsh landscape. The girls thought they were going to have fun making a movie. But Meyer's movies were anything but fun.

There would be a lot of tension on his sets because the conditions were so primitive. Russ loved women, but the women had to have big boobs. And they had to display them. He liked to show a woman as a work of art. But women were also brutalized in his films.

Russ convinced me to do what is easily the most embarrassing moment of my film career. He talked me into running naked, except for my boots and hat, straight at the camera. If you ever have the misfortune of seeing yourself doing what I did, you'd never do it again. And I didn't.

I played a crooked sheriff in this movie. There were some dangerous scenes on this shoot. I did one scene in which an Indian was supposed to miss me when he shot at me with a handgun, filled with blanks. When the Indian shot at me, he didn't miss me, and the blank in the gun came out of the barrel and hit me. It was only a wad of paper, but it hit me hard and knocked me down. The impact caused my shoulder to start to bleed. Russ couldn't care less as long as the scene was finished. Russ was just happy he got it on film.

Before the movie was completed, I got to meet the famous movie critic, Roger Ebert. Only then, he wasn't so famous. One day, I asked Russ about the chubby little guy who was on the set. Russ says to me, "Some kid from a big Chicago newspaper, and I may need him someday." That "kid" was a future Pulitzer prize winner.

Russ ended up hiring Roger to write a treatment for a story. He paid his airfare and flew him to LA. Roger later told me Russ picked him up at LAX. When Russ noticed that Roger wasn't carrying a typewriter, he flew into a rage. He yelled at him, "You're a writer. Plumbers carry tools. Carpenters carry tools. Where is your tool?"

Russ insisted that they get a typewriter. Since it was Sunday, the only typewriter that they could rent was one that typed huge letters. Because of that, the treatment Roger typed became a stack of papers a foot high. When they went to print shop to get it copied, Russ stared at the printer, and stated, "Don't say a damn word!" Russ and Roger were friends for the rest of Russ' life, with Russ even attending Roger's wedding.

After *Cherry, Harry and Raquel* was released, Russ told me the movie made "us" a lot of money. I corrected him and said, "It made YOU a lot of money, not us."

The money that Russ was making did not go unnoticed by the studios. In 1970, 20th Century Fox brought him in to produce films at their studio. The first movie he did there was *Beyond the Valley of the Dolls*. This was a spoof of the 1967 film, *Valley of the Dolls*. Roger Ebert, now a good friend of Meyer's, wrote the screenplay. The film makes fun of the 1960s rock music and film world. I had the part of Baxter Wolfe in this movie.

Needless to say, the atmosphere at a major studio was a lot different from working on the run in the desert. When the movie was complete, Russ had editing control. Despite the fact he made a lot of cuts, the movie still got an X rating. Fox didn't really care, as the film was one of the top grossing movies of the year. The critics savaged the film, including Gene Siskel. Of course, Siskel later had a TV movie review show with Ebert which lasted until Siskel's death. Recently two critics picked that film as one of the best 10 films of 1968-1978 era.

In 1975, I did another film with Russ called *Supervixens*. In this film, I was the star, playing macho cop, Harry Sledge. This movie ends with an incredibly brutal scene. I still cringe at the sheer intensity of the violence. I kill the female star, first stabbing her and finally electrocuting her in a bathtub. A lot of people in this business remember me for this scene and this role. Kevin Thomas, the critic for the *Los Angeles Times* stated: "Truly one of the most impassioned expressions of the battle of the sexes ever filmed." He compared the bathtub favorably to the shower scene in *Psycho*. When Russ was honored by The British Film Institute, the scene was praised as "brilliant action satire."

The film was a huge hit, grossing $17,000,000 (a *lot* of money in 1975). Considering it cost $220,000 to make, Russ proved sex and violence are a profitable winning combination.

Over the years, I have been questioned about the Russ Meyer films in a way that implies I should be ashamed of them. I'm not. They saved my ass. Jonathan Demme saw me in *Cherry, Harry, and Raquel,* and he later told me that made up his mind to use me in his future films. John Landis saw me in *Supervixens,* and then put me in *The Blues Brothers.*

Russ was a man whose tastes were excessive, whether it was films, big breasted women or food. A number of years later, I met with him at a very fancy restaurant on the Sunset Strip. We were meeting with two German film distributors, supposedly to raise funds for a film project.

I told Russ I didn't understand why this was necessary, since he was wealthy, with more than enough money to finance his own films. The answer was simple. Since WWII, he hated the Germans. He just wanted to have a great lunch and stick the Germans with the bill.

We started lunch by ordering shrimp cocktail. When it arrived, Russ got very upset. There were five or six shrimps in a small container. He called the waiter over and, very intently, told him, "See this table! I want it covered in shrimp." For the next few minutes, several waiters dumped shrimp on the table, until one fell on the floor. Russ looked up, and said "Stop."

Needless to say, the Germans were ill at ease at this whole display. I leaned over to one of them, and told him not be upset, Russ simply had a shrimp fetish. I continued, "All will be well, once he grows tired of eating shrimp." Sitting back I was fascinated by the whole scene, while our guests squirmed under this barrage of insanity.

I remember another restaurant incident, which occurred at the celebrated Musso and Frank Grill on Hollywood Boulevard in Hollywood. Russ never carried any cash, but he had an account at Musso and Frank. I would usually meet with Russ and his old Army buddy, Jim Ryan. Normally Russ would pick up the check and put it on his account. Once in awhile, he'd go into a tirade, saying Jim and I were taking advantage of him.

Jim would try to remind Russ of the tremendous profits he made from our labors over the years. Russ would then pay. I recall one time when Raymond Burr was within listening distance of our table, when one of these tirades occurred. Raymond was quite amused. Russ turned to Burr and yelled, "Mind your own business, you fat ass." Raymond blushed purple, and disappeared into his martini.

I never worked in another Russ Meyer film after *Supervixens*. But I stayed friends with him the rest of his life. On his 70th birthday, Russ came up to my ranch with Jim Ryan. Before he arrived, I went into

Bakersfield to make an unusual request. I went to the local bakery to ask that a cake be made that would look like two large breasts (two of Russ' favorite things). At first, the baker refused. But I convinced him to make a cake with two large hills, supposedly because the hills had special meaning to me. When I got home, I added a cherry on each, for the nipples. Seeing this beautiful cake, Russ broke out into a big smile, and expressed his gratitude.

Unfortunately, he developed dementia later in his life, and then passed away with Alzheimer's disease. Since his death, it has become fashionable for critics to recognize Russ' cinematic talents. It has been said that he is one of the only true auteurs of American film. I don't know about that but, over the years, I have been told by younger directors that they hired me because of my association with Russ Meyer.

Rock Hudson

In 1970, I was leaving a cast party at 20th Century Fox (for one of the Russ Meyer films made under the Fox banner) with another drunken actor, attempting to leave the "lot." A backlot on any studio is a confusing and spooky place in daytime. After dark, it is another matter altogether. Being intoxicated only intensifies the situation. Stumbling from one set to the other we eventually crashed through a wall and into or onto a set where Rock Hudson was filming the TV show, *McMillan & Wife*. There was a very hushed silence as all members of this film crew stared with shock, then anger as I tried to grasp the situation with a pickled brain. The First Assistant Director finally came out of shock and began a verbal attack aimed and me and my new friend, which reached a crescendo unheard of since Neanderthal days.

It finally dawned on me that my partner and I had breached a barrier that was heretofore considered inviolate. No one is supposed to ever enter a "Hot" set. To do so is running the risk of banishment from the establishment, especially a set occupied by the star Rock Hudson.

Let me preface this next scene by saying no one (that I know of) ever had a bad word to say about Hudson. Just as the First Assistant Director was going for the kill, that is "banishment," from the 20th

Century Fox lot forever, Rock walked over and laid a hand on the Assistant's shoulder. He said, "Take it easy. These guys are actors having a good time and I don't think they intentionally interrupted our set." Mr. Hudson was actually highly amused and suggested they all take a break, repair the set damage, comprised of a giant gaping hole, which would obviously be very expensive to repair. He asked my pal and me to accompany him to his dressing room.

He offered us a drink, asked our names and seemed genuinely concerned and interested in our well being. After putting us at ease, and even further into a coma, he had an assistant lead us out and back to the party we had accidentally left. Why we had wandered off, I shall never know, but we had managed to "crash" Rock Hudson's evening work. I'm sure he found it refreshing. There's nothing more boring than to be grinding out some mundane scene at 3 a.m. on a back lot of a studio.

Streets of San Francisco

In 1975, I flew to San Francisco from Los Angeles. I had gotten a part on the TV series *Streets of San Francisco*, which starred Michael Douglas and Karl Malden. Of course Karl is the Academy Award winner from *On the Waterfront* and *A Streetcar Named Desire* fame. Douglas later went on to win an Academy Award himself, as an actor (Wall Street) and as a producer (*One Flew Over the Cuckoo's Nest*).

Streets of San Francisco was a cop show, with Karl and Michael playing detectives. The scene I was in took place in a prison, and I was a police official. It was my job to present a criminal mugshot slide show to the assembled law enforcement people. Unfortunately, I was left to "cook" all day in a trailer.

An actor gets cooked when he waits a long time before he gets called to go before the cameras. In this state, the actor gets too much time to memorize his lines, resulting in his inability to remember his lines. Sounds bizarre, but it happens to the best of actors.

I finally get called to the set. In the scene Michael is on my left. He's very aloof as I'm brought in. Karl is on my right and he is friendly as he introduces himself. Those two have been working all day. I am nervous and sweating. I have three or four lines as I showed Karl and

Michael many different mugshots.

As I started to click the pictures to move on the slide machine, I couldn't remember my lines. Somebody in the crew laughed, and I froze. No one came to my rescue. Everyone, actors and crew, are watching this dumb actor being exposed. In the background, one of the grips starts to giggle. It seemed that this was going on for five minutes. Finally, Karl yelled at everyone, "Hold it. Cut it out." He turned to me and says, "Kid, let's get out of here."

We stroll out of the set, and go to his dressing room. He looks at me and starts, "Calm down kid. This is all bullshit. Screw those people out there. Don't worry about it. I've acted with Buddy Brando. Everybody goes up sometime. I'm on your side. Everybody will be on your side or I will kick their ass off the set." When an actor "goes up," his mind freezes because he's spent so much time waiting to say his lines, he can't remember them when he finally has to say them. He gets "cooked."

Together we go back to the set. Karl then addressed everyone on the set, "Give this guy some respect. He was cooking for seven hours. The first son of a bitch opens his mouth or snickers, I'll kick his ass back to LA. If you think you could do better, get up here."

He turns to me and says, "Kid, you say those lines. If you need cards, use them. Don't worry about it." He meant that I could use index cards with the lines on them.

Then they started the scene again and I did my lines perfect. I'll never forget what Karl did for me the rest of my life.

Baa Baa Black Sheep

In 1976, I was "assigned" a role on *Baa Baa Black Sheep*. Based on the book by WWII Marine Corps flying ace, and Congressional Medal of Honor recipient, Greg "Pappy" Boyington, it was a story of fliers with behavioral problems stationed on the South Pacific. I played Major Red Buel. I got to know the real Pappy pretty well, as he was a technical advisor to the show. I asked Pappy once, if there was such a man as Red Buel and he answered "If not, Charlie, there should have been." Pappy was the first of two Medal of Honor winners I came to know in my lifetime.

Robert Conrad was the star of *Black Sheep*, playing Pappy. He was a former boxer, who became a big TV star, acting in such shows as *Wild, Wild West*. There were other actors of note: John Larroquette, Dirk Blocker, the son of the Dan Blocker, who played Hoss Cartwright on the TV hit show *Bonanza*, and James Whitmore Jr., whose father was obviously James Whitmore, the longtime great character actor.

Bob Conrad was not a man to be trifled with and he ran a tight ship. We got along fine after we beat the shit out of each other for what seemed like an eternity in a boxing scene, which was supposedly scripted. How do you "write a boxing scene"? Just type "fight," I guess. But no one said "cut" to us, and the "fight" was continued on, much to the amusement and delight of the bored extras and sundry actors. Since I was taller than Bob, it was fairly easy to stay out of his reach. But since he was the star, he had to win. TV or no TV, in those days, stars always won. John Wayne saw to that. But as a result of that scene Bob and I became friends and still are to this day.

Our semi-permanent air base was an abandoned airstrip called Indian Dunes, located in Valencia or Santa Clarita, California. The script called for authentic aircraft. They used WWII fighters, Corsairs. By that time, there were only eight or ten of these fighters still in flying condition, and these were privately owned. If ever a man had an expensive hobby, this was the way to pay for it as the Corsairs were on a "rental" basis. Their owners got to dogfight (make believe) to their heart's content. Just sitting in one of these beasts with the engine at full throttle made one's blood turn hot, igniting a savage instinct to "kill." No wonder fighter pilots are a breed of their own.

One fine day the "company" was having lunch, when an unfamiliar noise in the distance caused everyone to pause and search for the source. It was an aircraft. One of the Corsair pilots muttered, "That's a fighter." This aircraft was fast approaching at an alarming speed and altitude. This was not the terrible roar of a South Pacific Corsair, but the hum of a different tune. The entire movie crew watched with jaw dropping attention as a P4l Mustang screamed over a distant hill.

It skimmed the airstrip deck at 200 + mph, pulled into a near vertical climb, barrel rolled two or three of times for good measure. It circled around and popped down on the deck without even a screech. Hardened "grips" almost wept. The Corsair pilots seemed dumbstruck. How dare a Mustang invade their space!!! Everyone watched transfixed as the Mustang taxied up. The purr of the engine was like a tiger on the prowl. The pilot gently stopped the plane. And after making sure everyone's attention was caught, he cut the engine. Out stepped the pilot: it was Steve McQueen. Put that in your pipe and smoke it. In today's world, you'd say we were "Punked."

A couple of years later, I ran into Steve on Sunset Boulevard. By this time he was very heavy, and barely resembled the famous image we all know as Steve McQueen. I asked him if he recalled the incident at Indian Dunes. He nodded and smiled, saying, "I just wanted to meet Pappy Boyington."

A PR shot from the TV series, *The Oregon Trail* (1977).
From the author's collection.

Oregon Trail

In 1977, while I was still under the Hitchcock-Universal contract, I did a TV series called *Oregon Trail*. It was a western set in the 1840's. Rod Taylor was the star and I played a scout called Luther Sprague. Rod was an Australian, but he had become a big American star in the 60s, doing such movies as the classic Hitchcock film, *The Birds*.

They were shooting in Flagstaff, Arizona when I was hired. I flew in but there was no one there to meet me. I hung around the hotel for three days, when someone from the production staff approached me. They didn't realize I was there. He told me that they were starting to shoot the next day, and Rod wanted to see me right away.

I was taken to his room. With a crazy look in his eye, Rod held out his hand, "How are you, mate?" By and large, Rod had conquered his accent, but he would periodically lapse into it. We hit it off and drank through the night. We started to shoot the series the next morning.

Rod was a real hell raiser, along with some of the other actors and crew. After a while, Rod and the rest of us were banned from every bar in Flagstaff. One day, Leroy, a bar owner, approached Rod and told him, "I heard you can't get in any bars. You're welcome in mine." After we finished that day, Rod, myself, some of the wranglers and stunt

A shot from the set of the TV series, *The Oregon Trail* (1977). From the author's collection.

guys headed to Leroy's bar. It was a low life bar on the edge of Flagstaff. We walk in and Rod walks over to a TV on the counter. He picks it up and throws it through a window. Behind the bar, Leroy didn't miss a beat. He looks at Rod and says, "What will you have?" Rod laughed and that bar was our refuge for the rest of our time in Flagstaff.

One of the things they don't tell you about making a western is that it can be hazardous. We were doing a horse chase scene. We, the good guys, were chasing the bad guys. In a chase scene, the guys in front are in the danger zone. If a horse goes down or throws the rider, that rider is in trouble because he may get run over by the chasing riders. Well, one of our riders, Ross Dollarhide, Jr., got thrown and he was run over by the riders in the back, including myself. He got up and everyone thought he was ok. He went with us that night. He laughed with us and he ate and drank seemingly all right. The next morning, he was found dead. Apparently, he had suffered severe internal injuries.

Some scenes were filmed on a Navajo reservation. The Indian ruling council came to the producers. The told them, since the show was being filmed on an Indian reservation, they had to use real Indians on the horses in the scenes being done. The director asked them, "Can they ride?" The Chief says, "Indians and horses are like a handshake. You can't shake them." So the director put 20 young Indians on the horses bareback.

The director yells, "Action." There was a cloud of dust and bodies started to fall everywhere. When it was over there were 20 horses passing the camera, without any riders on them. Of course the Navajos were embarrassed, but they no longer rode a horse bareback like their ancestors. You need trained riders to ride without a saddle.

This scene reminded me of story told by David Niven. He was making *The Charge of the Light Brigade* with Errol Flynn in 1936. Michael Curtiz was the director. Curtiz came to the US from Hungary in 1919, but he still had problems with the English language. There was a scene where they needed 100 riderless horses to race past the camera. Curtiz yells to the wranglers, "Bring on the empty horses." Niven and Flynn started to laugh hysterically, which made Curtiz very upset. "Bring on the empty horses" was a "curtizism" that became a famous saying in Hollywood and was the name of one of David Niven's books (from "Bring on the Empty Horses" Coronet Books, © 1977). Well, as a result of the scene I had just witnessed, the phrase had a new meaning.

Some of the scenes for this series were done at the studio in LA. There was a campfire scene being done on a sound stage. Rod and I were supposed to ride our horses from outside the stage into the scene inside. Unwisely, we started to gallop while we were outside. Under the sawdust inside the studio, there was concrete. This is not good for the horses. Sure enough, as we got inside the horses skidded and fell. They took out the campfire and the cameras. One of the producers screamed that Rod and I would not be allowed back on the lot for our stupidity. The series was cancelled after 13 episodes.

Handle with Care

Afer *Oregon Trail* was cancelled, I signed up to do a movie with Jonathan Demme called *Handle with Care* (1977). Demme was a new, young director then. But he would go on to win an Academy Award (*The Silence of the Lambs*). This movie was the beginning of a lifelong business relationship and personal friendship between Jonathan and me.

The movie starred Paul LeMat. Some of the other actors involved were Ed Begley Jr., Bruce McGill, and Candy Clark. The story revolved around truck drivers and the new found use of citizens band (CB) radio by truckers. The scenes were filmed at night, some in the rain. It was the worst night shoot I was ever involved in. At that time, LeMat was ticketed to be a major star. Unfortunately for him, that never happened.

I played a character named Chrome Angel. It was a great role. I had to drive an 18-wheeler in this movie. When I had to drive by the camera, it was a major project to reshoot the scene. It would take about fifteen miles for me to turn the damn thing around. Periodically Jonathan asked me if I was drinking booze. He could smell alcohol on my breath, but there were no bottles in the truck. He couldn't figure it out. What he didn't know was I used the CB radio to call some of my new local friends. When I drove to the spot where I turned the truck around, waiting for me was a local truck driver. The local guy was giving me a shot of my favorite refreshment every time I showed up to turn around.

The next day, I felt bad. I went to Jonathan with an apology and I told him the story. He was not amused but we forged a strong bond of friendship as a result of this movie, and I worked with him many times after. Jonathan is the kindest man I ever met.

Handle with Care was my second film with Ed Begley, Jr. Ed and I would go out each day (or night if we were free) to party. In the first film I made with Ed, he was very shy, but not this time. During this shoot, I became a mentor, of sorts, to Bruce McGill. This was his first film, and he was very nervous. Up to then, he had been a stage actor, and wasn't used to the pace, down time and burst of intensity of film making. I tried to "show him the ropes," so to speak. He has told others that I was a great help to him in getting his film career started. Of course, he went on to great fame as "D-Day" in *Animal House, The Legend of Bagger Vance* and over one hundred movies and TV shows.

Big Bob Johnson
And His Fantastic Speed Circus

After I did *Handle with Care*, Paramount Television approached me about doing work for a proposed TV show called *Big Bob Johnson and His Fantastic Speed Circus*. When I was first called in to meet the producers, I just thought I was being interviewed as an ordinary actor. When they asked me about what directors I liked and what I thought of certain actors, it dawned on me that I was being offered the lead role in a TV pilot. If the network liked the pilot, this show would become a series. I'd have steady work with a steady income.

My character, Bob Johnson, was to be the leader of a group of stock car drivers that put on Joie Chitwood-type shows at county fairgrounds and racetracks. There would be a lot of auto crashes and stunt driving.

Maud Adams was going to be my female co-star. She was one of the most beautiful women in the world. An ex-model from Sweden, she appeared in three different *James Bond* movies, which I think is still a record. The producers actually asked me if I would accept Maud being in the series. I yelled back at them, "You gotta be kidding. Of course, who wouldn't?"

We were filming in Louisiana, and using New Orleans as our base. I was sitting by the hotel pool one day, when I see this black kid sneak in and dive in the deep end of the pool. I didn't pay much attention until I didn't see him surface. I got up, dove in, and brought him up from the bottom. I proceeded to pump the water out of him. He came to, got up and wandered off. There was no one around at the time (or so I thought).

A few days later I received a note in my hotel box, which invited me to a party in a certain section of New Orleans. Upon checking with the locals, I was told not to go there, as it was a section of the city that was off limits to whites. Now I have done four or five movies in that city. I am an honorary Captain in the Police Department, and I was never told about this certain section of the city.

I decided to go. At first I thought I would go with a cop, but the cop declined. So I took a taxi. The cabbie was nervous and asked numerous times IF THIS WAS WHERE I WANTED TO GO. The cab dropped me off just a few blocks from the French quarter. After a few blocks, I was surrounded and greeted by several well-dressed mulatto men. I was immediately put at ease, and was taken to a beautiful house. Escorted into the house, I was told to sit there, as I was a guest of honor. In a few minutes two very nubile ladies came and escorted me into this beautiful room. The VooDoo Queen of New Orleans smiled at me, got up and gave me a big hug.

Basically, she said she had been told what I had done. She knew I had pulled the black kid out of the pool. I said, "There was no one around." She said, "There is always someone around in the Quarter." I was wined, dined and assured I would be taken care of while in New Orleans.

Well, when they started filming the pilot, they used the director I suggested, Jack Starrett. Jack was a talented actor I had worked with before. But Jack was also a director. He directed a lot of low budget action films and episodic TV, like *The A-Team*. His most famous acting role was the bad cop in the first *Rambo*, where he unmercifully harassed Stallone's character, when Rambo was put in jail.

Unfortunately, the network didn't pick up the show as a series. It ended up being just another TV movie.

Thunder and Lightning

Another movie I made around this time was called *Thunder and Lightning*. Filmed in the Florida Everglades, it starred David Carradine and Kate Jackson. David was just coming off his *Kung Fu* TV fame. *Kung Fu* was a philosophical western which became a big hit during the early seventies.

When David arrived on the set, he was wearing no shoes, jeans, no shirt, accompanied by a dog held with a rope as a leash. In the fight scenes, David was using his Kung Fu skills but he wasn't pulling his punches. He was hitting the other actors with his hands and feet. That's painful, especially when you don't expect it. One actor, Ron Feinberg, says to me, "I've had enough of this shit."

The next time, Ron is in a fight scene with David, he hits David with a bottle right between the eyes. He knocked him out cold, but fortunately didn't cut him. When David woke up, Ron explained why he did. David learned a hard lesson.

One night David, some of the other actors and I were sitting around bullshitting. We were in the middle of the Everglades with nothing to do. We kidded David about the fact that he never seemed to have any money. He said he bought some cars and gave the rest to the Indians. We wanted to get to civilization, but unfortunately the production company didn't want us to go anywhere, so we had no car. David listened to our complaints and disappeared.

A few minutes later, we hear a horn honking. David hot wired one of the movie cars. We all piled in and we were off to Naples. I had a hell of a night. I woke up with a hangover, alone, with no money. I hitchhiked a ride back to the Everglades and made it back for the day's shoot. It was last time I did that on this movie.

When we were making the movie, we used air boats rented from the locals. One day they were putting a lot of equipment, including cameras, sound equipment, etc., on one of these boats. One of the local swampers warned them, "You're going to sink that boat." One of the Hollywood equipment guys replied, "We know what we are doing." I'm watching as five guys also get in the boat to operate all that equipment. Before our eyes, the boat starts to sink. Water comes up to their knees and awful lot of very expensive equipment was ruined. They should have listened to the swamper.

The director on this movie was Corey Allen. Corey started his career as an actor. He is most famous for playing the antagonist in the knife fight and chicken run scenes with James Dean in *Rebel without a Cause*. In our movie, he tells David to take the air boat and go up river, traveling away from the cameras. Corey instructed him to then make a right turn at the curve in the river.

Dave gets in and guns the boat up the river. He is going about 60 mph as he gets to the curve of the river. To our horror he doesn't turn to the right, but heads straight into the bushes, and the boat goes 20-30 feet into the air. David gets ejected from the boat. Needless to say, everyone was in a panic to see the star of the movie go flying. Fortunately a couple of the crew got to him. By the time they brought him back, he was alive, but with a few cuts and bruises. This can be a dangerous business. David learned a lot of lessons on this forgettable movie.

Budd Boetticher

Sometime around 1979, I had an opportunity to meet Budd Boetticher, who many regard as a brilliant director. He directed a lot of great Westerns during 1950s and 60s. His most famous movies were starring Randolph Scott, such as the great film, *Seven Men from Now*. His films tended to be more realistic than the usual Westerns of the period. A friend of mine introduced me to him. He lived in a condo community near San Diego.

By then he was in his mid-60s, with a very beautiful wife, as I remember. He was a classy guy, but paradoxically tough. The thing we talked about was horses. He loved horses. He took me to see five Portuguese horses that he owned. He worked them out daily. Since I knew nothing about this type of horse, he proceeded to show me how they were trained. We were at an arena, where he led each horse through their paces, by cracking a whip. The horses would leap into the air and seemingly, in slow motion, perform different movements. It was very impressive. This was a man with a strong personality.

We talked for a while about the animals and then the movies. I got the impression he had nothing going on as far as films were concerned. It then seemed that Budd wanted to prove something to me about his dominance of these animals. He led me to section of the stables where he kept a stallion. As soon as we approached, the stallion lashed out with a ferocity that scared the hell out of me. He smiled and said, "You must let the stallion know that you are not afraid of him, otherwise he will kill you." He then quickly entered the stall. While the horse went crazy, Budd calmly walked past the horse and sat down. For about five minutes, the stallion went through all kinds of menacing motions, but never touched Budd. I was terrified. I wouldn't have gone in that stall for a million dollars.

The stallion finally calmed down, walked over and lowered his head to Budd. He reached over and gently stroked the horse between the eyes. He then walked out of the stall. The minute Budd got out and locked the gate, the horse went berserk again. As the animal seemed to be pissed at me, I politely asked Budd if we could leave. Budd smiled and we left. Well, I didn't get a movie job out of it, but I did get a lifetime memory.

Melvin and Howard

In 1980, I got a part in a new Jonathan Demme movie called *Melvin and Howard*. It's a light hearted comedy, based on the story of Melvin Dummar. Melvin allegedly once found Howard Hughes wandering in the desert and gave him a ride to Las Vegas. Hughes was the eccentric, wealthy recluse who designed and built planes and was a Hollywood producer, among other things. The Bo Goldman script for this movie won the Academy Award. During the filming, I got to hang out with the real Melvin Dummar. He was quite an interesting guy, who told a great story.

I was excited to work on the movie because Jason Robards was playing Howard Hughes. Jason was not a big movie star, but he was highly respected among actors for his stage work, especially performing in various Eugene O'Neill plays, such as *Long Days' Journey Into Night*. Unfortunately, as he got older, he developed a bad drinking habit and producers didn't want to hire him. Then, he was involved in a bad car accident that did substantial damage to his face. He required a lot of reconstructive surgery. After the accident, the light finally turned on and Jason stopped the drinking and started to get work again. Fortunately for me, he was hired to do *Melvin and Howard*.

At this time of my life, I was into partying and having a good time. And after all, we were filming in Las Vegas. Therefore, I was told to leave Jason alone. Nevertheless, after I was sufficiently inebriated, I headed over to his room. I started to beat on his door. He yanked open the door and seemed to be pretty pissed.

After I told him that I was in the movie with him, he smiled and invited me in. He warned not to bring in any booze, as he didn't want to be tempted. Once inside, he told me a funny story about him and Robert Preston. They were both acting in plays in New York, Robards in the O'Neil play and Preston naturally in the musical, *The Music Man*. After the shows, the two went out together drinking. They got sufficiently soused that when they went to Robards' apartment, Robards' wife, Lauren Bacall, would not let them in the apartment. In fact, she slammed the door in the in their faces. Two of the biggest stars on Broadway were left on the streets of Manhattan, with no booze and no more money.

Filming in Vegas meant casinos had to be in some of the scenes. One night Jason and I did a shot where we walked through a casino. Now, keep in mind, anywhere else in the United States, when a film crew is filming a movie, it will draw a crowd of gawking spectators. But not in Vegas. As we filmed, people continued to throw the dice, play the cards, and work the slots, giving us no thought. They couldn't have cared less.

During in a break in the filming, a gentleman, who was obviously drunk, approached us. He looked at Jason and said, "Are you really Lee Marvin?" Jason replies, "No, I'm not, but he is," pointing to me.

The drunk looks at me and asks me who I was. I told him, "I'm

John Wayne." He didn't believe me because he said John Wayne was taller. I told him I didn't have my lifts on. He then said, "John Wayne doesn't need a lift. He has a chauffeur." Confused by now, the drunk staggered off. Jason was laughing so hard, he almost pissed in his pants. Over the years, whenever I'd see Jason, we would retell that story. Jason would say, "I'd tried to dump that drunk on you, but you bested me."

Jason was nominated for an Academy Award for his excellent acting in *Melvin and Howard*. During his lifetime, he won two Academy Awards and eight Tony Award nominations. Jason is gone now. He was a good friend. I got to work with him later again in the film *Philadelphia*. I considered it a privilege to have known Jason Robards and to have worked with him.

The Blue and The Grey and Gregory Peck

I was playing a Union officer in the TV mini-series called *The Blue and the Grey*. The year was 1982.

One day we were told that Gregory Peck was going to be arriving to play Abraham Lincoln. Peck was a legendary Hollywood film star. Peck was up there with Gable, Bogart and Cagney. He won an Academy Award for playing attorney Atticus Finch in *To Kill a Mockingbird*.

Since this was to Peck's first TV experience, we were told not to speak to him or bother him in any way since he was a *movie* star. This didn't seem to go to well with my fellow actors, Sterling Hayden, Warren Oates, Rip Torn, or Lloyd Bridges, but not much was said about it. I was just glad to be there to see Gregory Peck in person. Or so I thought.

Finally the big day arrived, and Mr. Peck ambled from his dressing room. He took a chair on the set several feet away from the rest of the cast. He "was" Lincoln. Sterling Hayden then said to me, "Charlie, aren't you from Kentucky?" I said, "Yeah, why?" Hayden continued, "Well, wasn't Abraham Lincoln born in Kentucky?" I said, "Yeah, I know a lot about Lincoln. We used to go see his log cabin on school trips all the time; we really studied Lincoln." Sterling asked, "Was the mole on his face on the right or left side?" I thought for a moment, and glanced at Mr. Peck, who was within earshot. I noticed the mole the makeup people had applied to his face was on his left cheek. I quickly caught on to the game and replied, "Right cheek." "You sure?" said Hayden. "Absolutely," I said, "know just about everything about old Abe."

We all waited to see what the reaction from Mr. Peck would be. He carefully reached up to check the mole on his left cheek. Then very regally, he got up and headed back to the makeup trailer. No one said anything. It was all too surreal. Mr. Peck arrived a few minutes later with the mole now placed on the right cheek. Then, after he had settled in, I said, "You know Sterling, I was wrong. The more I think about it, it was on his left cheek." Would he take the bait? Peck glared at me, but again got up, and headed for the dressing room presumably to have the mole switched again. We just all sat around and looked at each other in astonishment, too scared to laugh. He had gone for it and I knew I was going to be in deep shit with this man for the rest of my life.

Later that night in the bar, I'm drinking with Hayden, Warren, Rip, Stacey Keach, and some other guys from the movie. We see Peck easing his way toward us. Sterling says, "Here he comes, get ready." Peck eased up to me, looked deeply into my eyes and said, "Who are you?" I didn't know what to say. I told him that I was just playing a general in the movie. He said, "Are you really sure about the mole?" I assured him the mole was in the proper place. He then said, before moving on, "I don't like you." I assured him the feeling was mutual.

Later on two or three buses of school children from the local schools came to meet the "real actors from Hollywood." As usual, Mr.

Peck had his place under a tree sitting there regally as Lincoln. The children came clamoring out of the bus running toward the set. I was standing several feet behind Mr. Peck, who rose to greet the children. He stretched his arms out to greet these kids, who ran right by him and started jumping all over ME. Mr. Peck glanced back at this scene and stalked off to his dressing room.

That night, again in the bar, same situation, Mr. Peck warily approached me. "Who are you? Why did those children love you and not me?" I said, "Mr. Peck, I am a regular on a TV show called *BJ and the Bear*, and lots of kids in the US watch that show. I play a character called Hammer, and that's probably why they hugged me and not you. We also have a chimp on the show whose name is 'Bear,' and kids seemed to love that combination of actors and monkeys." He looked at me as if I was crazy, and muttered, "A monkey? They love you because of a monkey? But I'm a movie star. They're supposed to love me." I didn't have an answer for that one and he walked away muttering, "Monkeys. I don't understand."

I continued to haunt this man, it seems. A few years later, I was a guest of the Governor of Kentucky for the Kentucky Derby. At a black tie dinner in the Governor's mansion, I ran into Mr. Peck again. "What are you doing here?" he asked. I explained that I was from Kentucky and the Governor had invited me. He stated, "But you're the guy who works with monkeys." I answered, "Well, not anymore, that series ended." He looked at me sternly, "You know, I don't like you." What could I say?

On Derby day, Peck watched me with this horrified look, as I boarded the Governor's helicopter for a trip to Churchill Downs.

Peck had to take a limo. At the Derby, I was sitting at the Governor's table with several celebrities. Peck approached me again. "How come I didn't get to ride in the helicopter to Churchill Downs?" he asked. I simply said, "Like I've been telling you for years Mr. Peck, I am from Kentucky." I don't say these things to put Peck down, I say them because that's how this bizarre relationship started and ended.

Sterling Hayden was another notable actor who worked on this film, loaded with talent. He made some great films (*The Asphalt Jungle* and *Dr. Strangelove*). But he made a lot of mediocre films. Sterling was the most intense man I've ever been around on the set. One day we were waiting around for a shot to be set up. His intensity was so powerful it made the rest of us feel uncomfortable. It was like waiting for a grenade to explode. One day, he did explode. He leaped to his feet and yelled to no one in particular, "God damn it, I just can't visualize the rest of my life not being able to sit outside a café in Paris with a drink." Then it was over, he sat down, and seemed to calm down.

Sterling loved the sea and owned his own schooner. There were periods of time when he quit making films and decided to just go sailing. His autobiography, *Wanderer*, highlights his adventures sailing the world's seas. We didn't say a lot to each other, as he was not an easy man to talk to, but we had a kind of unconscious social connection, which is hard to explain. In acting, you tend to meet some unusual personalities, and Sterling was certainly one of the more unusual persons I have met in the movie business.

The A-Team

During the 1980s, one of the most popular TV shows was *The A-Team*. It was an action adventure series on NBC. The A-Team was a renegade group of former soldiers, who went about the country righting societal wrongs that they encountered. The show was a weekly demolition derby, punctuated by cartoon-like violence.

The leader of this group was Col. John "Hannibal" Smith, as played by veteran actor George Peppard. At one time, Peppard was a big matinee film star, in such great films as *Breakfast at Tiffany's* and *The Blue Max*. As his film career waned, he found success in television.

Mr. T played an expert mechanic, named "B.A." Baracus. Mr. T played the character "larger than life." He became a national sensation. At that time, you would see Mr. T toys everywhere.

I appeared on several episodes, as Army Col. Briggs. The show was a "live action cartoon," made up of explosions, crashes, stunts, and general mayhem. But it did have some dialogue. On one show, I had a problem with my lines, causing me to have a disagreement with the script director.

I decided to talk to the star of the show, George Peppard. I went to his motor home on the set. He invited me in and we discussed the issue. His reaction was, "Look, this is my show. I'm proud to have you on it. I'm glad to see that when you have a problem that you came to me." George was very sympathetic. But nothing changed, except I was fired by the producers, who didn't appreciate the disruption. Even with that history, the producers still had me back for other episodes

I had very limited experience with Mr. T. He was not a very warm person. I tried to start up a conversation with him, but got nowhere. I did have a fight scene with him, and neither of us held back. At lunch time, he would eat five peanut butter sandwiches, and then retire to his trailer, listening to taped sermons from his Chicago pastor.

The last time I saw George was in 1994, at a charity celebrity event in Dana Point, California. This gentleman came up to me and greeted me like we were friends. I didn't recognize him. Then he said, "Charlie, don't you recognize me? It's me, George Peppard." I apologized, feeling like a jerk for not recognizing him. We had a good talk, reminiscing about the past. Unfortunately, he died a few weeks later, as a result of complications from treatment for cancer. George was a good man.

Rambo: First Blood II

I've known Sylvester Stallone since I did a *Kojak* show back in 1975. Those were his pre-*Rocky* days, when he was just a struggling actor. Back then, Sly was in the same boat as me, doing bit parts and heavies on TV. He complained to me that he was in the depths of despair: "I'm going to be playing these goons for the rest of my life." But that all changed when he made *Rocky* in 1976. By 1984, he was a huge international star, not just for the various *Rocky* movies, but also for the initial Rambo film, *First Blood*.

The first *Rambo* movie had been big money maker and crowd pleaser in 1982. The studio wanted another *Rambo*. Stallone started to work on a script and put together a cast. Word in town among agents was that Lee Marvin had the part as Murdock, who was Rambo's antagonist and the chief civilian intelligence officer in charge of the mission Rambo was going on.

I was with the Meyer Mishkin Agency, which represented Lee Marvin, Charles Bronson, Claude Akins, Jack Palance, and James Coburn. Don Gerler was an agent with this agency and he was one who got me the audition with Alfred Hitchcock. I wanted the Murdock role so I figured I better change agents. I hired Sam Gores as my new agent. I told him I wanted the Murdock role. He told me we had a problem since Lee Marvin had the role.

I decided to take things in my hands. First, I got a copy of the script. I then went over to the studio where Stallone was working. I found Stallone's office and went in. The secretary was not amused. I told her I wanted to read for Murdock role. She said the roles are all filled. Just then Sly was walking down the hall to the bathroom. He stopped and said hello to me and wanted to know why I was there. I told him I was interested in the role of Murdock. He told me to go back to his office and I could read for the role.

I read some lines. He turned to me and told me I would have to put on 20-30 pounds. He said "You'll need a gut." He turned to one of the producers, who was sitting in his office, and said "Get Lee Marvin and pay him off." I figured I better track down Lee, who I knew. He was fishing in the ocean off the coast of Australia. He didn't even re-member he was in the movie. He said he had no problem with me tak-ing the role as long as he got paid. Marvin got paid and I got the role.

I went to Mexico for a couple of weeks and gained 30 pounds. I am not usually that aggressive in trying to get a role, but I knew it would be a good role for me. And it was. A lot of people remember me as Murdock from *Rambo II*.

Working on a movie with Stallone was a truly unique experi-ence. Usually when you are making a movie, if there are changes to be made in the script, it requires all kinds of meetings. But with a Sly movie, where changes have to be made, he just goes into his dressing room and writes the changes. No need to consult writers, producers or agents. Sly is the boss. He makes the decisions. It's a very efficient way to make a movie.

A movie set can be very mysterious and snooty. There is a well-accepted pecking order. Of course, at the top, you have the major star, Stallone, and then important supporting actors, such as Richard Crenna. I was somewhere between those two and the stunt guys. Stallone and Crenna were housed in private villas away from the nightly activities of the hotels. I stayed at a "not so private" hotel. But I had no complaints. When the film was finished, I got third billing in the credits, behind Stallone and Crenna, my highest billing on a major, big budget film.

In the movie itself, I play the villain. I am the chief CIA operative who sends Rambo out on a dangerous mission to look for American POWs in Southeast Asia. But after Rambo leaves on the mission, I change the plan without telling him. Basically, instead of giving him help, I leave him high and dry. Needless to say, Rambo does not appreciate my skullduggery. The hero triumphs without my help and comes back to get me. Sly machine guns my office to pieces and then scares the hell out of me by throwing me on my desk, and sticking a huge knife perilously close to my face. Scary but not real, of course.

It was a good movie and audiences loved it. When the movie opened, it was as close to stardom as I will get. I went to the World Premiere in Hollywood. As I got out of the limo, the waiting fans went crazy. I will never forget that phenomenal feeling, as I strode onto the red carpet.

What a natural high. From playing Adam on *Star Trek* to the red carpet for *Rambo II*.

Filming Overseas

After *Rambo: First Blood II*, I had a little pull, which helped; but in order to actually get an acting job, I had to figure out a way to find the right people to give me a job. For some reason, it occurred to me that I should attend the AFM (American Film Market) in Santa Monica. I rented a room and simply sat at the bar for a few days.

The foreign film market was long past the "La Dolce Vita" days of the 60s. It had more or less been reduced to very low budget films, cobbled together by several financial interests from Israel, South Africa, Italy, etc. My advantage was *Rambo*, which had become a worldwide hit.

Most of the films I participated in during those days were a mixture of many actors from several different countries. Some of these actors, in years past, had probably achieved a certain amount of fame. Others, who knows? Though the foreign market was looked upon as the "grave yard" of a Hollywood film actor's career, I didn't see it that way. To me it was a chance to follow my wanderlust, doing what I do best and support my family.

Thanks to Jonathan Demme I was able to keep my head respectfully above water in films such as *Handle with Care, Silence of the*

Lambs, Miami Blues, etc. Then off I would go to such countries as England, Spain, Bulgaria, Russia, Argentina, Peru, Dominican Republic, Mexico, the Philippines, just to name a few. I was always paid. One-half up front, first class plane ticket, and, if I survived, I'd be paid the remainder of the deal when I returned. I suppose the most important thing I learned was what a great country we live in. All the people who gripe about the USA should spend some time in the hellholes of Africa, or any other so called "third world" countries.

While waiting to start a film in the Philippines, I was sitting in a hotel bar in Manila, waiting and watching people. When you travel alone, and the plane lands, one steps into a very unfamiliar world. Is anyone going to meet me? Will they know what I look like? The sights, smells, and uncertainties are almost overwhelming. However, somehow, it all seems to work out. Strange languages, different looking people, coupled with the knowledge that if something went wrong, nobody would ever find me, was soon shaken off by the excitement of the challenge ahead.

After an hour or so at the hotel bar, a very striking lady approached me. I could tell she was American. She was smiling, and I was feeling very lucky thinking I was going to have this beauty as a companion. My ego was shattered when she told me she was the wife of one Fred Williamson, known in the States as "The Hammer," who played in the National Football League. This knowledge ended all illusions of my perceived fantasy, thus I shifted to my best behavior, since I did not want to be "hammered" in Manila by "The Hammer."

Mrs. Williamson (Linda) told me that this day was Fred's birthday. She invited me to his party, to be held at some other location. Of course

I said yes. Being alone, without the chance of ever seeing another American was a horrible thought. Besides, I would get to meet Fred.

At the party, Mr. & Mrs. Williamson and myself bonded rather quickly as the other guests spoke mainly Italian. I consumed too much wine. Fred carried me on his back to the hotel, thus starting a friendship that continues to this day. I am probably the only guy that ever held on to the Hammer's back for more than twenty minutes. We met several times again in different places. Fred did me lots of favors and we worked together later in several films. I have had the pleasure of working with several athletes. Sonny Liston was a great pal, and obviously good to have on one's side in bar fights. There were others: there was Jim Brown, Marvin Haggler, Sugar Ray Leonard, Shaq O'Neal, John Matuszak, André the Giant and probably others I have left out, but have not forgotten.

André The Giant

In the late seventies and early eighties, I was a regular on an NBC TV show *BJ and the Bear*. Interestingly enough, I played a character named "Hammer." I didn't think I had to ask Fred Williamson for permission to use the name. That's been a long time ago but just the other day, some guy at a gas station yelled, "Hammer!" I nearly fell over, but was glad he remembered me after all these years.

I was on the lot at Universal waiting for a car to pick me up and take me to the set of *BJ and the Bear*. There was this giant human being standing there. I do mean *giant*. He stood seven feet tall. It was the professional wrestler known as André the Giant. I had been told he was to be guest starring, but to see this man in person, "up close" so to speak, was rather unsettling, to say the least. Before I could say anything, he stuck out this giant "ham" of a hand and introduced himself. Since I had not done my homework on professional wrestling, all I knew was that he was a wrestler. And after sizing him up, I had no doubt.

André was born in France, and became very popular here in the US when Vince McMahon of the WWF got hold of him. He dominated wrestling for fifteen years. He had many great wrestling matches, including one of the most famous of all time with Hulk Hogan. In the middle of all of this, he started a career in films and TV.

After waiting a little while, our "ride" came screeching to a halt and out jumped a young third assistant director in a car no larger than a Yugo. He stared at André and said, "Get In." André replied, "I can't get in, would you like me to try and GET ON TOP?" The kid finally got the message. I told him to get something big enough to haul our guest in style. Pretty soon he came back in a pickup truck. André hoisted himself into the bed and I crawled in behind him.

When we arrived at the set, the amused crew grew silent as André got out and loomed over them. I simply said, "Guys, this is André the Giant, and he will be my best friend for the duration of this week's episode." Everyone treated me very kindly the next several days.

One night during the *BJ and the Bear* shoot, André (in the front seat) , myself and Bill McKinney (from *Deliverance*) were out in my old Buick. Because something was wrong with the license plate, we got stopped by a North Hollywood cop. After looking at the occupants, he actually drew his gun. The cop asked, "What is that thing in the front seat?" Our driver says, "That's André the Giant, sitting with Charles Napier and Bill McKinney, the guy from *Deliverance* that had his way with Ned Beatty." The cop recognized us and yelled, "Jesus Christ, you're a bunch of freaks. Get out of my side of town NOW!" We obeyed and immediately left the area.

André became a good friend. One time he was a guest in my home. He told my son, Whit, "One of the reasons I like hanging out with your Dad, is that people stare and bug him as much, or more, than they bother me." At that time, I was just coming off my appearance in *Rambo II*, and was at the height of my fame. He was truly a gentle giant. He suffered a lot from back pain during his life. At times the pain was so great that it robbed him of his strength. André loved living in the US, and owned a ranch in North Carolina at the time of his death in 1993.

Instant Justice

Early in 1986, I got the opportunity to make a film in Spain called *Instant Justice*. This was an action thriller. It starred Michael Paré and Tawny Kitaen. Earlier in the 80s, Michael had become a star in the cult classic *Eddie and the Cruisers*. *Instant Justice* sticks out because I met a wonderful man named Eddie Avoth.

Eddie was a great character, who grew up in South Wales. During the 1960s he was a great boxer, being crowned British and Commonwealth Light Heavyweight Champion. His boxing career lasted for nine years, with a record of 44 wins and 9 losses. After he retired from the ring, he became owner of the famous celebrity restaurant "Silk's" in Puerto Banus, Spain. In between all of this, he tried acting. And that's how I met him. Eddie had a part in this movie.

One night, he and I were out drinking. We joined two women for some friendly drinks. During the night, we had to get up to relieve ourselves. While we were gone three Middle Eastern men had taken our places. When we came back, Eddie didn't say a word; he walked up to the three gentlemen and, one by one, physically removed them from the premises like ragdolls. As physically imposing as he could be, he was gregarious and a great story teller. He counted the great British actors, Richard Burton and Stanley Baker, as close friends and he could regale you with anecdotes about both. I haven't seen Eddie since that movie but the thought of him strikes joy in my heart.

Instant Justice was a forgettable film. I'm not sure it was ever released in the US. I remember Tawny being a spitfire from hell. Michael was a great guy, but his career never took off like I thought it would. Today he lives in Europe. One good thing came about because of this film. That's because I brought my manager, Roger, with me. That turned out well because he negotiated some deals for me to make some films in Italy. The first paid me thirty five thousand dollars for two weeks work in Rome. Not bad.

I ended up making a couple of films in Italy and Europe in the 1980s and 1990s. No one remembers the films. But I always like to be paid to go on vacation in Europe.

The Outlaws

In 1986, Universal was trying to put together a cast for new Western series called *The Outlaws*. They originally targeted James Whitmore and Johnny Cash as the stars of the show, but that didn't work out. They decided they needed Rod Taylor to lead the series.

I had been a friend of Rod since our days on the TV series *Oregon Trail*. Universal knew that, so Nick Corea, the show's writer, and some studio executives came to see me. Nick, as well, had known me from my *Oregon Trail* days. My visitors told me that they had a part for me in the series, along with Richard Roundtree. But they had to have Rod. They wanted my help.

I warned them that Rod was living comfortably in Palm Springs and he was still mad at Universal because of the cancellation of *Oregon Trail*. When that series had ended, we were told by studio execs that Universal didn't want Rod or me back on the lot at any time.

Then Corea hit me with a bomb, "*The Outlaws* starts filming in 48 hours." I told him to get me a couple of limos and get me and his group to Palm Springs right away. I added, "I'll take over from there." I brought my guitar.

When we got to Rod's beautiful home, we were greeted by a butler. He let us in and took me to Rod. Sitting at a bar, Rod looked up and said, "Did you bring your guitar?" I nodded and told me to go get it. "Play me some songs. I'm in a bad mood." He smiled at me, "Tell those assholes to come in too."

I played some songs. Believe it or not, Rod cried. He's very sentimental. I then introduced Corea and the studio execs. I told him Universal wanted him to star in the TV series, *The Outlaws*. Rod countered, "What about James Whitmore?" Rod was no dummy. He had heard the rumors. He looked at the group and said, "Have a drink and I'll think about it." The execs spoke up in unison saying, "We don't drink." Rod glared at them, "Well, you do now."

Rod thought it over and then the haggling started. I had to call Rod's business manager and the finances were worked out. Rod drove back with me to LA. We partied all night. The following morning we started to shoot the series.

The series had a strange premise. In the 1890's Rod was a Texas sheriff leading a posse that was chasing a gang of bank robbers. Caught by a freak electrical storm, Rod, his posse and the gang were propelled into the future—1980's Texas. Bizarre.

While the series lasted, I struck up a friendship with Richard Roundtree, who played a character called "Ice McAdams" on the show. Tree, as his friends called him, had become famous in 1971, as the movie's first black private detective in *Shaft*. I've always had an affinity for minorities. Minorities can be mined for beautiful thoughts, feelings, and experiences, not available to white people.

Tree and I became close and he told me things I doubt any other white person has ever heard. He was and will always be my brother. The last time I saw Tree was on a film called "*Steel*," which starred the basketball all-star, Shaq O'Neill. One night we sat in Tree's dressing room, sharing some scotch. We talked about life. We both dropped our guard. There was no black, no white, just two men sharing their thoughts about parents, women, fame and other subjects.

We talked through the night, and discussed about how close we came to fame. Me, with *Rambo II*, and Tree with *Shaft*. He had created the character Shaft. It was his. Later he would have to suffer the indignity of someone else (Samuel L. Jackson) appropriating his character in the 2000 version of *Shaft*. When someone takes a character you created, you can't help but feel your soul has been stolen; but then we work in a world of illusion. Life moves on.

CBS cancelled *The Outlaws* after one-half season.

Radio Shack

I had become a friend of Freddie Fields. He was the agent who founded CMA, the famous talent agency. He represented Paul Newman and Barbra Streisand. He became a producer and then was made President of Paramount Films.

One day, I get a call from Freddie. He asked me to get over to the studio lot right away. Naturally, I went immediately to the studio. I was shown in to his large, ornate office. Freddie was in a meeting with Richard Brooks, the director and writer. Brooks was an Academy Award winner for writing Elmer Gantry, and directed *In Cold Blood*, *Cat on a Hot Tin Roof* and *Blackboard Jungle*, among others. Brooks had no idea who I was.

I asked, "What's the problem?" Freddie looks at me and points to a side office. He tells me, "Those guys in there are from Radio Shack of Texas." He then looks right at me and says, "Aren't you a red neck?" I laughed and told him I was from Kentucky. Apparently Radio Shack and Charles Tandy (the founder) had invested in a Fields movie, which turned sour. He begged me, "Go in and straighten it out." I said, "You screwed them, right?" Forlornly he talked low, "Well kinda, yea." I agreed to go in and talk to the Texans.

I walk in and there are six men in the room, all wearing cowboy boots. Tandy speaks up, "Who the hell are you?" I asked him who he was. Very firmly he replied, "I'm Charles Tandy. I own Radio Shack. That son of a bitch in there just fucked us out of a lot of money." I looked him in the eye and said, "Mr. Tandy, I'm just a dumb actor. But I'm here to tell that you can forget about whatever you think they owe you. Just take it. Go back to Texas. You've been screwed over by Hollywood because that's the way it happens out here."

He looked long and hard at me. The others looked to see if he would laugh or punch me in the mouth. Finally, he laughed, "You have a lot of balls to come in here and tell me that shit." I reiterated, "That's the way it goes down here."

Tandy surprised me with the following statement, "How would you like to work for Radio Shack?"

"What do I got to do?"

Quickly, he replies, "Be our spokesman."

Just like that I was a spokesman for Radio Shack. My agent, who was supposed to get me commercial work, was incredulous when I told him. For the next five years, I worked for Radio Shack at $75,000 a year.

Blues Brothers

In 1980, I got the role of Tucker McElroy, the lead singer of a country and western band in the infamous movie, *The Blues Brothers*. John Landis, of *Animal House* fame, was the director. I saw him on the Universal lot. He came up to me and tells me, "I saw you in that Russ Meyer film (*Supervixens*). Go tell your agents to do whatever they have to do. I want you in this movie." My agents did their job and I was in *The Blues Brothers*.

Of course, the stars of this opus were John Belushi and Dan Aykroyd, who reprised the musical characters they created on the TV show, *Saturday Night Live*. Belushi was a great comedian, who branched out successfully to comedic acting. There have been many stories written elsewhere about the rampant drug use on this set. I won't contradict those stories, but I didn't let that situation affect me.

I had a scene with Belushi, usually called the "motor home" scene. In the movie my country band, the "Good Ole Boys," was supposed to play some club in Illinois. The Blues Brothers band was looking for work so they pretended they were my band. The club owner hired them thinking they were my country band. I played the leader of the band. After the Blues Brothers finished a set in which our band was supposed to play, our band, in a motorhome, pulled up to the club .

The Blues Brothers. **From the author's collection.**

We find out what happened, and I was supposed to confront Belushi. But we had a big problem. Belushi kept calling the scene off, saying he wanted to do it later. After this happened a couple of times, I went to see John. I asked him, "Why can't we do the scene? What's the problem?" Belushi looks up at me, "I think you're going to kill me." I assured him I wasn't going to hurt him.

He then told me that he saw me play the homicidal Harry Sledge in Meyer's *Supervixens*. In that movie he saw the scene where I kill a woman in a bathtub. After we drank some champagne and I once again promised I wouldn't hurt him, he said, "Let's do it." We then went to the set and did the scene.

This movie contains one of the most famous lines I ever spoke in a movie. Jake (Belushi) tried to stop Tucker (me) from going into the club. He said I needed a union card to go inside. Pressing my face up against his, I told him, "You're gonna look pretty funny trying to eat corn on the cob with no fucking teeth." People still quote that line to me to this day.

Here's a side note on *The Blue Brothers* movie: When this was being made, I thought it was a real piece of crap. Of course, it turned out to be one of the biggest hits of 1980 and of all time. A lot of times an actor has no idea how a movie will do when it hits the theatres. That's true more times than most. When you're doing your scenes, you're concentrating on your job, saying the lines and moving where you're supposed to. You don't really pay attention to the rest of the scenes in the movie. You have no idea how the complete movie will come out, or how audiences will react to it. I was wrong big time on *The Blues Brothers.*

Interestingly enough, many years later, Russ Meyer prevailed upon me to set up lunch with John Landis. I did, but the lunch didn't go well. It seems John had ordered a copy of Russ' autobiography from Russ' office (which was quite long at three volumes). Although John paid $300 for it, he never got his copy. After John raised this subject, the conversation deteriorated and the lunch ended. I had to pay the bill.

Married to the Mob

Another movie I did with Jonathan Demme was *Married to the Mob* (1988). I was not originally cast for this film. One day when I visited the set, Jonathan asked if I would get made up as a hairdresser. He wanted to run a scam on his star, Michelle Pfeiffer. In today's language, she was going to get "punked." He has one of the assistants call her to the set to get in the hairdresser's chair. I was an outrageously dressed hairdresser. She arrives on the set. She didn't know who I was.

I pretended to work on her hair. I began to yank on her hair. She started to squirm in her chair. She was obviously uncomfortable. She looked at Jonathan and he finally yells at me to stop. She realized something was up and screams, "This is a setup." We all laughed and so did Michelle.

Jonathan was so impressed by my little stint that he had the screenplay revised. I now had a part as the hairdresser for Michelle's character. I played it over the top. It was one of most outrageous roles, for which I got many compliments.

Charles Napier in military uniform from a 1980's TV show.
From the author's collection.

War and Remembrance

In 1988, I got a part as a Lt. General Smith in the TV miniseries about WWII, *War and Remembrance*. I was really there to keep Robert Mitchum happy. We were old friends and drinking companions. The producers figured I could keep an eye on Bob. The movie was shot in England. Everyone knows Mitchum was a major movie star of the 1940s and 1950s, who was now making a living doing miniseries on TV.

Bob and I were out one day, camping out in an English bar in Cambridge. The great English actor, Trevor Howard, came into the bar. Being a longtime friend of Bob's, he came over to us. He sat with us and we drank for several hours, telling old war stories. Surprise of all surprises, we got drunk and a little loud. Some women were sitting nearby, and one of them came over to complain.

Trevor looked at Bob and me, snorting, "I'll handle this." He then turns to the lady, and in that beautiful English accent, scolds her, "Look, you bitches, this is Robert Mitchum from the USA. He is a big movie star. I demand an apology from you right away." Of course the women were very apologetic to Bob and then all of them asked him for his autograph.

Not long after, the booze got to Trevor, and he fell off the bar stool. We picked him up and put him in his limo.

This movie was a good payday for me. Even though I was listed as a US officer in the credits, I was really a glorified baby sitter for Bob Mitchum. I might add I did a good job as an actor *and* a babysitter.

Over the years, I kept in touch with Bob. He never changed his lifestyle. Heavy smoking and drinking remained a big part of his life. In 1996, it finally caught up with him. He was diagnosed with emphysema. A few months later, he was told he had lung cancer.

During the summer of 1997, I got a call from Bob's son, Chris. He told me his father was dying from the cancer. He asked me to come to visit his Dad at his home in Santa Barbara. He told me to bring some fun with me. When I got there, I was taken aback by Bob's appearance. He was thin, bony and very sickly looking.

I snuck some booze into his room. Watching him drink, he seemed to genuinely enjoy it. Every once in a while, his wife, Dorothy, would look in and then turn around and leave.

Bob's frustration with his condition exploded one time, when he took his walker and hurled against it the wall. This was a man who was not going to go quietly.

Those few days in Santa Barbara became a blur, filled with booze and bullshitting. When it was time to leave, there were no hugs or sentiments between the two of us. Bob just said, "Get the fuck out of here." I replied affectionately, "Ok, fuck you too, Dad." I got up and left. That was the last time I saw him. He died shortly thereafter.

Grifters

A lot of times you will do a film because of a great script, or the money, or because you haven't worked for a while. I did the movie *The Grifters* (1990) because I wanted to work with Anjelica Huston, an Academy award winner and daughter of the great director John Huston. When I heard she was in the film, I agreed to do it without even seeing the script. My mistake. This was a film loaded with talent: Huston, John Cusack, Annette Bening, and J.T. Walsh. Martin Scorsese was co-producer, and narrated the film.

I never heard of the term "grifters," before this movie. Basically grifters are con artists. Guess what? In the script, my character gets conned by J.T.'s character. In real life, I was the one that got conned. The only reason I agreed to do the film was the chance to work with Anjelica. Let's just say I was misinformed. By the time I reported to the set, and saw the final script, all of my scenes were with Annette Bening. A good actress, but not Anjelica. I was very disappointed, but I was contractually bound.

This turned out to be good film, receiving good reviews. I only worked on it for a few days. I did enjoy hooking up with J.T. Walsh. He and I had previously done several films together. J.T. was truly one of Hollywood's greatest character actors. When he died at an early age in 1998, Jack Nicholson paid tribute to him in one of his Academy Award speeches.

Red Necks in Love

Many years ago, Buck Flower and I wrote a screenplay called *Red Necks in Love*. Buck was an actor, writer and a longtime friend of mine. It was a story about a law school graduate from Boston sent to a rural area filled with red necks. Jonathan Demme read the screenplay and liked it. He decided to help us try to get a studio involved.

Demme set up a meeting with Dawn Steel. She was President of Columbia Pictures, the first woman ever to head a major studio.

Demme made a sales pitch for about an hour, with me and Buck sitting there quietly. Steel listened intently and then said, "We might be able to do something. Of course these men here are not stars. I don't want them. They only way they get paid is with a deferment."

Deferred payment means Buck and I wouldn't get any upfront money or a salary while the movie is made. We would get paid down the road, if there were sufficient revenues. In other words, we MAY get paid in twenty years.

Buck got up, walked over to Steel and pointed to her, "Look, Lady, I'm over 50. I ain't waiting. So stick it up your ass. We're out of here."

We left. Of course, our screenplay never was made into a movie. But Buck did make a great exit. Ironically Buck and I didn't give up on the story and *Red Necks in Love* was published as a novel in 2002. You can get it on Amazon.com, if you like.

Charles Napier with Anthony Hopkins.
Copyright notice: "*The Silence of the Lambs*
© 1991 Orion Pictures Corporation. All Rights Reserved."

Silence of the Lambs

I have worked with Jonathan Demme many times, but one of the most famous movies I did with him was *Silence of the Lambs*. It was based on the Thomas Harris best seller, and featured a character who will live on forever in movie folklore, Hannibal "The Cannibal" Lecter. This film ended up winning five Oscars, and it deserved all of the accolades it received. It starred Jodie Foster and Scott Glenn as the FBI agents in charge of the case, and Anthony Hopkins as Hannibal. Hopkins, one of the great actors of our time, won the Academy Award for this role.

I played a cop, Lt. Boyle, and I had several scenes with Hopkins. At first he seemed to be a bit standoffish. One day I saw him sitting alone off to the side of the set. I sat next to him and introduced myself. He told me he was aware of my work. I found him to be a regular guy and very friendly. He would talk about sports, news, or whatever.

Hopkins is truly an amazing actor. He was never nervous and he was always ready for the next scene. He would be talking to me about some mundane subject, and then get called to set. When he got before the camera, he would go right into that diabolically evil character, rip off eight pages of dialogue, and come back and talk to me like he just went for drink of water.

It was something to watch firsthand, how he skillfully portrayed the insanity behind the Hannibal character. Demme told me, "How do you direct that? I just let the guy go." Watching Hopkins act is something I'll never forget. No method acting, just *incredible* acting.

If you've seen the film, you know my character (Lt. Boyle) gets killed by Hannibal and his body gets hoisted up to hang from the ceiling. There my "body" was made to look like a flying angel or devil, if you will. Before they shot the scene, Jonathan told me I had to fly to New York, so that they could make a full body cast of me (it would be what you see in the movie hanging from the ceiling). Needless to say, making this cast was a very uncomfortable process to go through. In order that I could breathe, they put two straws up my nose. All in all, I handled it pretty well. Anything for the profession and all that bullshit.

When I finally saw the figure on the set, it looked like a monstrosity. There were two FBI observers on the set. One of the agents saw the figure and exclaimed, "Oh, my God!" Jonathan told me later that I could have the figure. Unfortunately the production company, Orion Films, went into bankruptcy after this film. So I couldn't get the figure and it probably is lying somewhere in a warehouse. I still wished I had it.

The fascination with *Silence of the Lambs* endures to this day. I recently did a documentary for cable TV, dedicated to telling the story of the making of this film.

Philadelphia

In 1993, I played the trial judge in another great Jonathan Demme movie, called *Philadelphia*. This was the story of an up and coming lawyer, who works for a large, prominent law firm in Philadelphia. As the lawyer battles AIDS, he is fired by the firm.

The cast in this movie was filled with past and future Academy Award winners: Tom Hanks, Denzel Washington, Jason Robards, Joanne Woodward, Jonathan Demme (as director), among others. Renewing our friendship from *Melvin and Howard*, I hung around with Jason during the filming.

It was a pleasure working with Jason again. We spent a lot of time together. Jason was a true artist when it came to acting. He knew his craft. He was very helpful to me with the script. During the trial, I had a long speech. Jason made me do it over and over. I could not have done it without him. I had to do that speech in front of all those Academy Award winners in a courtroom scene. I did the speech and I think I did it well. They all sat there and paid attention to me. Sadly, that speech was cut out of the final version of the film.

This was a very difficult movie for Tom Hanks to do. He wasn't very social on the set. He was losing weight every day. In the movie, he is gradually dying before your eyes. It was a very physically and mentally demanding role. Of course, his efforts paid off, as he won his first of two consecutive Academy Awards. Take it from me, as someone who saw what Tom went through up close, he earned it.

Sometimes reality intrudes on illusion. One day, while still in my judicial robes, I went outside Philadelphia's City Hall to catch a smoke (I still had that bad habit then). I was standing near an entrance when a well-dressed gentleman (a lawyer, I presumed) approached me. He warned me that it wasn't very safe for a judge to stand outside City Hall like I was. I thanked him for the advice and went inside. I found the wardrobe woman and gave her the robe. I went outside and finished my smoke. No one bothered me.

I have one other interesting story about this film. Jonathan and I were standing in a building, on a balcony overlooking the set that was used that day. Harry Belafonte had been someone's guest on the set. We saw him as he headed for a door to leave. Jonathan called out to him, "Hey Harry, give me the 'Banana Boat' song." Without hesitation, Harry broke out into his most famous song. I shall always remember the verbalization of that beautiful voice echoing through the deserted building. He probably never sang for two people in his life for free, but he did for us. Jonathan could con God out of his sheet.

Tyson the Movie

HBO produced a film about the life of Mike Tyson, the heavy-weight champion fighter. Appropriately it was called *Tyson* (1995). The story, as originally written, had former great boxing champs Jack Dempsey, Joe Louis and Rocky Marciano portrayed in flashback scenes. I was hired to portray a younger Jack Dempsey.

At that time Tyson was still a formidable force in boxing, even though he had started to lose a few fights and had a lot of legal problems. But a young Mike Tyson dismantled each and every fighter crazy enough to get in the ring with him. He did it with a savagery not seen since Rocky Marciano in the late 1940s and 50s. Cus D'Amato, his mentor and manager, was played by George C. Scott.

On the set, I could not resist sneaking glances at the great George C. Scott. This actor was a man's man among actors. Mr. Scott had the gonads to turn down an Oscar for best actor in *Patton*. He was either insane or he received bad advice. Looking back, when Scott turned down his Oscar, he evidently made a wrong move, as he never made another "A" list film. Maybe that's what he was trying to do with me, in a made-for-cable TV movie.

At any rate he suddenly got up and headed in my direction. I almost froze with fear. What the hell had I done? Mr. Scott had been known to have a very short fuse. He was feared and given a wide berth among all human beings on a movie set. My fears were defused when he stuck out his hand and said, "I'm George C. Scott. I like your work. You remind me of a younger me." After a firm handshake, he turned and walked back to his chair. I felt as if I had been anointed by the Pope.

Suddenly the director, a woman named Uli Edel, looked at me with a different light. Having had Mr. Scott's blessing made me swell with undeserving importance and I proceeded to "act my ass off" as he nodded approval. As one could assume, everyone treated me with undue respect the rest of the day.

Our little "bond" formed, we then went on to a scene in a church. I was seated two or three pews behind Mr.Scott. The scene began. I gave him my line and his "cue." There was silence. Scott never responded. The director was too terrified to say cut. Mr. Scott turned furiously around and glared at me and said, "Are you going to give me the cue or not"? I lamely screwed up my courage and muttered, "I did George." Nobody, I guess, ever called him by his first name. But he calmed down and said, "Forget it. I don't want to do this shit again."

Getting an acting job is fraught with many perils, twists, and turns. The part of Jack Dempsey was no different. I accepted the role. Who wouldn't want to portray Jack Dempsey? There is no feeling akin to knowing you have a "job." There's always the possibility that "something" will happen to rain on your parade, so one is usually in agony until the word "print it" is announced. My fears were confirmed when my agent first called me about the part and announced I would have to use a New York accent. Since I do not do New York accents, I told him to forget it and to turn it down. After much lamenting and haranguing he turned the role down, and proceeded to tell me how stupid I was. I informed him that "they" would go out and try to find a real boxer, who couldn't "talk," much less memorize a page of dialogue.

They called back and the agent shrewdly asked for twice the money. Again they searched every gym in town and could find no boxers equipped to beat the living shit out of a movie scene. I've seen grown men shake with fear when staring down the lens of a camera. The producers came back to me.

I only had one day to perform my role. It was a fairly long monologue, which I was able to wrap my tongue around, with a fair amount of confidence. I've had a running battle with screenwriters since I had enough courage to challenge them and their written word. Writers should be "made" to read their masterpieces out loud in front of real people before forcing them on actors, who are asked to repeat their words in front of a camera.

The dreaded "script supervisor" is always lying in wait for the actor to skip or twist these written pearls of wisdom. The attitude of most screenwriters is that their words are "carved in stone," and you'd better not change them. But I have challenged various writers on many occasions. Sometimes I have been successful, sometimes not. But that won't stop me.

When *Tyson* was shown on HBO, my part was edited out. Being cut out of a movie in the final edit is an occupational hazard. You can't control that situation. You have to grin and bear it. You move on. But if you did a good job, it does bother you.

The Cable Guy

In 1996, I got to work in a Ben Stiller-directed black comedy, *The Cable Guy*. The story about a cable TV installer starred Jim Carrey and Matthew Broderick. Carrey is a very interesting man. He first made a living doing comedy; very physical comedy. He then turned to acting, becoming a major movie star with *Ace Ventura*.

He is very shy off camera. But on camera, the transformation is incredible. That is the mark of a true actor. He had the explosive power of Robin Williams. Jim has a good sense of humor and also sense of loyalty.

My role was small, and word got out that the producers were going to cut my role. Jim and Ben Stiller interceded and kept me on board for the full shoot. That was a nice Christmas present.

Matthew Broderick was also a star on this movie. Broderick was famous for such films as *Ferris Bueller's Day Off* and *The Freshman*. I had a scene with him where I played a cop. In the movie Broderick played a poor schmuck who befriended Carrey. Carrey's character gave Matthew a large screen TV and a lot of audio equipment. Carrey had set Matthew up, since the stuff was stolen. I played a cop and it was my job to arrest Matthew for receiving stolen property.

Matthew was sitting in an office at a business meeting, and I had to come in and arrest him. When we rehearsed the scene, I told him I would grab him, stand him up and press his expensive face into the table top. He was instructed three different times to turn his head sideways so his nose would not be flattened. He must have been more worried about his makeup, because, when we did the scene, he didn't turn his face sideways. Splat went his nose into the table. He actually started to bleed. He howled and bitched for a few minutes. Finally, we did the scene again, and this time he turned his face sideways.

The next day Jim Carrey walked up to me at the food table. He giggled and he shook my hand and said, "I heard you guys did a number on Matthew Broderick yesterday." He then turned and walked to his expensive motor home, laughing.

Based on my conversations and experience with Jim on this movie, I liked the guy. I know he has a reputation for being weird, but I didn't see any of that. He was very timid. He's a brilliant actor. He's also the most underrated actor I have ever been around. The movie did not do well as far as gross receipts go. I don't think the audience was ready for Carrey playing such a dark character.

Rod Steiger

Rod Steiger! I wish there was something good or nice I could say about this person. In 1999 I had come into New Orleans to film "something" called *Cypress Edge*. Arrived at the hotel and was taken to someone's room where I was not introduced to anyone. My character was called "Riley." Mr. Steiger was in the process of browbeating two of the young leading actors. Here is the very man I had seen years ago in *On the Waterfront*. Here was the man who played Brando's brother, and the scene where the infamous words were said, "I couldda been a contender." Steiger won an Oscar for *In the Heat of the Night*.

Steiger was told that my character was named "Riley." He never learned my real name.

Rod was in the process of screaming that this script was a piece of shit and he needed to fix it. Although I hadn't been told, I calculated quickly that we were to start filming the next morning. Instead of panicking as usual, I decided to listen to what Steiger had to say. No one was writing down his suggestions, which made this whole farce much more interesting. I had slowly figured out over the years that the "less" one says in one of these potboilers the better one will come out, as if coming out of one of these "potboilers" is even worth noting. After all, one acts to work, not work to act, at least that's what I thought. Still do.

Strother Martin, of *Cool Hand Luke* fame, was once asked if he would work for scale. He replied, "If I can get it." I sorta feel the same way. All of us actors should all bend over and kiss our ass. Especially those "few" who have survived this war. And a war it is, has been and always will be. No matter how "cheap," no matter how "crude," the camera can make grown men quake and scream with terror. Those who claim no fear are lying.

I was once under the "desk" with Tim Robbins, while filming a scene from *Austin Powers*. Robbins had fear in his eyes. I know, because I was there. I too had fear, but was interested to see that he, too, was not exactly on solid ground. Where was I? I must say, there's nothing like having to make an appearance by shooting out from under a desk in an *Austin Powers* movie. You'd better be damn funny!!!!! A lot is riding on this little move, believe it or not. It is a business, damn it.

Back to *Cypress Edge*. The next morning, of course, started with the usual confusion associated with just about any movie. Egos clash. Cameramen keep tweaking. Wardrobe people flutter about like shot quail. Makeup people are slathering on the "paint" (they seldom return after the third day). Hair stylists comb your head into little ridges (no one EVER combs their hair like that). Extras muscle for position. On and on until finally someone croaks out, "Action." Since Mr. Steiger had changed everything the night before, no one knew what to say except him. He raged on for several seconds and waited for an answer from "someone." No answer was forthcoming. After checking with the terrified "script girl" (a good person to know well), Steiger harangued the cast for "not knowing their lines." My "lines" had been shitcanned (thank God). I could only watch with amusement as this "piece of shit" sank slowly. Somehow, someone, probably the 2nd Assistant Director, shouted "cut" and we moved on.

Next day, Brad Dourif was attempting to do a scene with Mr. Steiger. We were all on board a good sized yacht, floating on the then-placid waters of Lake Ponchetrain. Mr. Steiger whispered to me, "Watch this." When the camera filmed his "close up," Steiger spit in Dourif's face. Mr. Steiger beamed. No one else moved. I walked out of the scene and stood on the poop deck. Mr. Steiger came out and said, "What did you think of that?" I will not say what I told Mr. Steiger but I didn't hold back anything. Of all the discourteous acts I have ever seen committed in all my years of acting—that was the absolute crudest of all. Fortunately, I never worked with Steiger again.

Charles Napier with co-author, Dante W. Renzulli, Jr.,
on the set of *Annapolis* (2006). From the co-author's collection.

Annapolis

Disney hired me to do a movie called *Annapolis*, about the training of plebes (first year Naval students) at the Naval Academy, to start filming in September of 2004. I was playing Superintendent Carter, the commanding officer of the facility in Annapolis, Maryland. But Disney had one big problem. The film was supposed to be done on location at the Academy. After the naval honchos read the script, they informed Disney that they would not allow the film to be shot at the Academy, as long as the script remained as it was written. It seems they were scenes involving fraternization between a plebe and an officer. That's a no-no in the naval world.

So the movie had to be shot somewhere else. They found Girard College in Philadelphia. Girard had classic buildings which resembled the buildings at the Academy and Philadelphia had some streets and other type of buildings which resembled Annapolis. This is a practical problem that many studios have when making a movie. Sometimes you can't do it at the location where the events occur. The problem can be costs, climate, destroyed buildings, or script issues, as in *Annapolis*.

I was happy to be back in Philly. It was the site of one of my most notable films, *Philadelphia*. The two stars of the film were young and up-and-coming: James Franco and Tyrese Gibson. Franco began on TV, doing shows that appealed to young people. His most famous movie role was a recurring character in The *Spider-Man* films. Tyrese started out as a singer, and then branched out as an actor. He had quite a following. Disney saw this movie as vehicle to market two young stars to a young audience.

The script involved obvious story lines about conflicts between the plebes and the officers who were training them. But the movie did not really involve ships and the sea as you would expect. Believe it or not, it was a fight movie. Each year, one of the biggest events at the Academy is the boxing competition known as the "brigades."

Franco played a plebe, who had been an amateur boxer before attending the Academy. Gibson's character was an officer, who was the reigning Academy boxing champion.

When you make a boxing movie, there is a lot of choreography involved. In other words, the actors have to be trained in the various moves they have to make in order to make the boxing action look real, without the actors actually hitting each other. Of course, as the film is being shot, over a long day, an errant punch may connect once in a while.

Among the stunt men and the boxing trainers hired for the movie, Franco had the reputation of training very hard, and had become a passable boxer. Gibson had a different rep. He didn't put in the time Franco did in training. In fact, on some long shots, the director had to use a stunt double for Gibson. Tyrese just didn't have the correct technique down. The double in those shots was an actual boxer.

We did the big championship fight scenes at The Blue Horizon, which is a legendary fight venue in Philadelphia. It was more of a fight club atmosphere, as opposed to an arena. One day in mid-December, we gathered for filming the climatic scenes. For whatever reason, no one was smiling that day. Part of the problem is the extreme cold, the lack of heat in the building, the sheer boredom of doing the same scenes over and over the previous days.

Franco and Tyrese start to film the fight. About an hour into the filming, Franco hits Tyrese hard over the left eye. Tyrese yells and the boxing trainers come running into the ring. You could see his forehead start to swell. They apply some ice to his head. Both actors leave the ring and go to the food area.

At that point, in front of the crew and extras, Tyrese yells at Franco about the punch, warning him not to do it again, otherwise something was going to happen. Needless to say, the set is very somber after this. Nobody jokes around. It's all business. I see the director, Justin Lin, talk to Tyrese for about five minutes.

They start the filming again. But Franco and Tyrese never look at each other when the camera is not rolling. There was real tension in the air. After a while, the director calls for a 30 minute break to cool things down.

Around noon, we go to lunch. But the big topic of discussion is Franco and Tyrese. Everybody walks around like they were walking on glass. After lunch, they start to film the fight again. At about 4:00 pm, Tyrese throws a punch which hits Franco hard. He screams at Tyrese. Tyrese yells at Franco: "This is supposed to be a movie." Apparently, Franco thinks Tyrese threw the punch on purpose because of the incident this morning. Franco yells back at Tyrese: "Some of us are trying to make a good movie." They glare at each other and move toward each other. Tyrese throws his mouthpiece away and says: "Watch yourself playboy." It looked like we were going to have a real fight.

The boxing trainers and director jump over the ropes into the ring as they see their movie about to explode in their faces. The two actors are separated and both are hustled off the set. I turn to one of my fellow officers and say: "What the hell do they expect? These actors are making a boxing movie. You're going to get hit sometimes."

There are more discussions with the director and assistants huddled together. No more fight scenes today. First Assistant Director Vince Lascoumes comes to us in the officer's box. He tells us that we are to film a scene with the officers next; that cameras are set near us and we are all lined up.

Chi McBride is standing next to me. He is annoyed because the director and Vince aren't sure how they want to do the shot. Vince asks Chi to give him a moment to think the shot out. They had really planned on doing Tyrese and Franco the rest of the day, but now they couldn't.

Chi looked over to Vince, who was standing about eight feet from us, and yells at him, "We're not your fuckin' problem." Vince glares back at Chi and says, "Right now, you are my problem." Chi literally screams back, "I'm not the fuckin' problem. You've got another problem you have to deal with." At that point Vince's eyes stared back at Chi with frozen eyes. Chi continued to stare back for about five long seconds and finally says, "Don't make me the fuckin' problem." During this whole discourse about a fucking problem, I was standing next to Chi and a few feet from Vince.

After some continued glaring, and staring. Chi and Vince walked away. You could tell Vince was seething. During the filming of the boxing scenes, he was the man in charge. Chi had just challenged him in front of the other actors, extras and crew. By this time a lot of us knew that Tyrese was the problem Chi was referring to, but you don't humiliate a boss like he just did in front of all of those people.

The film only has two days to go. So the next day, when we get to the set, one of the officers tells me Chi was released overnight, as a result of his confrontation with Vince. Over the years, I have learned that you have to watch where and with whom you take a stand. The Disney people didn't hesitate to act. And they did. Overnight they hired a double for Chi. Chi had no more lines, so that wasn't a problem. They just kept Chi's double out of any close shots.

I'd like to tell another story about this movie. When you work a movie, you get to know the people who work on the movie with you every day, whether they are the other actors, the crew, the producers, etc. Most of the time you never hear from them again, unless you do another movie with them. On this movie, I met the co-author of this book, Dante W. Renzulli, Jr.

Dante was an extra, who played one of my naval officers. In the movie, you usually will see him standing at my side when I was in a scene. We developed a friendship during the shooting, just talking during the breaks or eating lunch. In real life, he is an attorney, practicing in Chester County, Pennsylvania. After the movie wrapped, we continued that friendship. Out of various conversations, letters, tapes and e-mails, the idea for this book came about. So even though *Annapolis* did not do well at the box office, I gained a lifelong friend.

Curb Your Enthusiasm

In November 2006, my agent asked me to come to LA for an HBO comedy show called *Curb Your Enthusiasm*. I had never heard of the show but it was a big hit and had won many awards. The star and chief writer was Larry David. Although I didn't know the gentleman, he was famous for being a co-creator of the TV mega hit *Seinfeld*, which he also produced and wrote. Of course, *Seinfeld* is regarded as one of the two or three best shows ever done on TV. As a result of syndication of the show, David is an extremely wealthy man.

The unusual part of *Curb Your Enthusiasm* is that it is improvised. There is an outline of the action in the scene but there is no script. Actors are trained to recite the words given to them in a script and to move about the set as directed to. Improvisation on a set, with cameras rolling, is not something most actors can handle. You have to have supreme confidence in your acting skills and your own intellect. Thinking fast on your feet is an absolute requirement. It is quite a challenge.

As I enter the audition room, I notice that the room is full of a lot of flunkies. In the middle is a slight bald man with an extremely red face and a crazed grin on his face. He is introduced to me as Larry David and I shake his hand. I am given the outline of the scene. I am a barber and Larry comes to my shop for a haircut. I have a son named Bart, who has a wife named Betty, with whom he has nine children. Betty has just had a miscarriage.

We start the scene. I pretend to cut his hair, that is, what little there is of it. We banter back and forth, improvising as we go along. Then he makes an insulting remark about my son and his wife. It was something about too many kids in the world. I stop and pretend I'm finished. I then ask him if he wants me to put some powder on him. He mumbled yes. I started to towel the powder on him gently but then, in a quiet rage over his insult, I started to hit him with the towel. Unfortunately I hit him hard, and he cursed. The scene stopped. I apologized and we shook hands. I left, quite frankly thinking I blew it.

A few hours later I get a call from my agent: "They loved you. You do the scene next week." You never know in this business.

The day of the shoot, I report at 8:00 AM, and I am taken to an actual barbershop in LA, which is closed so we can film the scene. When I am first brought to the set, I meet Larry's friend and manager on the show, Jeff Garlin. He is a large man and his part in the scene is very small; basically he just sits there, waiting for his turn for a haircut. I see Larry buzzing around, with three producers at his side.

Finally Larry comes over to me. No handshake, no greeting. He tells me that we will do pretty much what we did the day of the audition, only longer. They use two hand held cameras. Because it's improvised, you never know what to expect. But the camera people do explain my limitation of movements, although it is not blocked in the usual sense.

The cameras start to roll. The ad libbing begins to come out of our mouths. I tell him that I was retired but I decided to come back to work, so I just bought this shop. Larry says he loves the old style barber shop, and the sound of the clicking of the scissors. I asked what he did for a living. He says he is a writer. I pretend I don't believe him. I ask him if he ever been paid for any of his writing. He tells me he wrote *Seinfeld*. I reply mockingly, "Yeah, sure." We talk a little more about his writing and writer's block. Then he makes his wise remark, about my imaginary son's family, elaborating this time, that there are too many people in the world. Larry shows little sympathy when I tell him how depressed my daughter-in-law is because of the miscarriage. I then stop, tell him I'm finished and start to powder his head with a towel.

Like before, I started out slow, but then I went into a rage. My rage was controlled but I really felt it. My physical moves were unrestrained. For real, I snapped the towel against his head, as he got out of the seat, on his back as he got up. I then followed him to the door as he ran out, all the time snapping the towel against his body. I then stop and looked around and point to Jeff, and say, "NEXT!" Looking shocked, Jeff holds up his hands and mumbles, "Pass." He then beats a hasty retreat out of the shop. End of scene.

The mood of the crew, producers and other assorted watchers was interesting. Some bent over laughing hysterically. Others were in total shock, as they couldn't believe I was beating up their boss, and who some call a comedic genius.

We did three takes, but I can tell you that the first take was as close to reality as an actor can get. An experienced actor will tell you that the more an actor repeats a scene the less likely it is believable or fresh. For a variety of reasons, both personal and professional, my emotions had been building up, and they came out that day. I have no idea where this scene fits into the show, but it will be remembered because it was that good. If I never work again, this was the way to go out.

In the three takes, I hit Larry a total of about fifty times. He never complained. But his head was filled with red marks. Most stars would not have tolerated what I did to Larry that day. Larry may be a comedic actor, but as a producer, he knew what he wanted that day, and he got it. After the audition, he knew he was going to suffer pain when we did the scene live. He was willing to absorb it because the scene required it. He couldn't use a stunt double. Despite all the flunkies around him, he had the final say. Larry David knows his business, and as an actor, producer and writer, he is one of the best I ever worked with.

When I was ready to go, I presented Larry with a special gift. A few days prior to the shooting, I had to repair a hose on my car. I bought a small finger size hose clamp, the kind with a screw on it in order to tighten it. It occurred to me that it would fit on your finger like a ring. I threw another one into a ring box. I called it the Bakersfield Redneck Engagement Ring. One size fits all; furnish your own screwdriver. To an old redneck like me, it was amusing. As Larry opened the box, he stared at it, not knowing what it was. Being from Brooklyn, and living in LA, he probably never even opened up the hood of a car. I told him my name for it. I said, "It's a joke, Larry." I didn't mean to embarrass him. Some in the crowd got the joke and laughed. The gag didn't have the payoff I wanted. As I was leaving I saw Larry slip my "gift" into his pocket.

The Goods,
Live Hard, Sell Hard

In 2007, just when I needed the work, I got signed to do seven weeks of work in a Paramount movie, *The Goods, Live Hard, Sell Hard.* Jeremy Piven was the star. A lot of the cast is young, but one person near my age is James Brolin, husband of Barbra Streisand. Some of the people behind the scenes are quite substantial in their own right. Will Ferrell, the famous comedic actor, is a producer, along with Adam Mckay, and Chris Henchy (Brooke Shields' husband). Although filmed in 2007 and 2008, it was not released until August 2009.

Jeremy plays a super duper car salesman. He's hired by Brolin, the car dealership owner, to save his failing business. I play a long time salesman, who is very rough around the edges. Jeremy has been in the film business for a long time for a relatively young man. He didn't really make it big till he starred in the HBO series *Entourage,* as Ari Gold the entertainment agent. He is a very fine actor.

During the filming I struck up a friendship with Ken Jeong, who also played a salesman. Although a very good actor, Ken was actually a medical doctor. While completing his residency in New Orleans, he started to pursue his love of comedy. He appeared in clubs there and developed his comedic skills. He became very successful and was lured to Hollywood. He appeared on many TV shows as a comedic actor and now is doing films.

Believe it or not, the movie opens with me in a fight scene. The director, Neal Brennan, couldn't believe that I would do my own stunts. I've been in the business a long, long time. A good portion of the TV shows or movies I did were action flicks. I learned over the years how to do the stunts. So when Neal needed me to do a fight scene, he didn't have to get a stunt double.

In this role, I play an old WWII vet, who also hates Japs and Jews. Brolin plays my boss. I got to spend a lot of time with James. One thing you don't bring up with James is Barbra. We talked about films, actors, politics, sports, but no Barbra. At the end of the day of work, I would remember that I had to go back to my small hotel room, and he went back to a palatial compound.

After we finished the film, I never heard much about it. But in November 2008, I got a call from the director, Neil Brennan. He invited me down to Paramount in LA for a private screening for the studio execs and their friends. I never like watching myself on the screen, but I went anyway. I knew I played my role way over the top and, guess what, I was funny. The Paramount suits seem to really enjoy the movie and gave me an ovation when I was introduced. Naturally it made me feel great. .

When the movie came out in 2009, the critics were not very kind to the movie. They simply didn't like the movie. But a lot of them gave me good reviews.

Variety announced, "Frankly, the movie gets its best comedic mileage from character actor, Charles Napier."

Old friend Roger Ebert wrote, "….it was fun to see Charles Napier, whose career started as a member of the Russ Meyer stock company, in a mad dog role that gets the film off to a rip-roaring start. He still looks like he could fight a wolf with a T-bone."

"Napier gives the most enjoyable performance, simply because it is clear what his crusty old salesman is all about. " *Blogcritics.org,* by Hombre Divertide.

"The funniest guy in the whole thing was Dick Lewiston (played by veteran character actor, Charles Napier)." *Kansas City Auto Examiner.*

"The few real laughs, all two minutes worth, come courtesy of Russ Meyer veteran, Charles Napier…..Napier connects the dots between economic disenfranchisement and subversive humor." *L A Weekly.*

I don't like to brag but I will. I did a good job in this movie, and many of the critics acknowledged it.

At the premier of *The Goods: Live Hard, Sell Hard* (2009).
With Will Ferrell (Producer of the film) and Dr. Ken Jeong (fellow actor).
From the author's collection.

This is a shot from TV show "Mission Impossible" (1969).
From author's collection. Show is mentioned at page 24.

The Slammer

O ver the years I have had some run-ins with the law. Unfortunately those run-ins have resulted in my spending a night or a few days as a guest of the government. Usually the event involved a liquid substance known as liquor.

In 1956, I was in the Army stationed in Augsburg, Germany. I'm not sure why I was I arrested. The only thing I remember is that we were in a nightclub and there were these tiny lamps on each table. John Gilman (another Army grunt) thought it might be fun to take the lamp shades off and crush them. It didn't take long for the German police to arrest us. I do remember this. We were housed in a dungeon for several days in a foreign country. Finally an Army Major shows up and we are released. He didn't say much about what the charges were. He just shook his head in disgust and dropped us back on the base. I got my ass chewed out by my First Sergeant because he had to make out the morning report. He was worse than the Germans. I felt pretty bad, of course, and stupid because I didn't do anything but watch, guilty by association. Never having been incarcerated in a foreign country, it was quite an eye opener for me.

Remember this was only ten years after WWII, and there were

members of the SS still lurking in the police force. In addition, there were rumors of a Russian attack at any time. But we were young and very excited about it all, until we had a talk with two men in our company who had served in WWII and Korea. After several days of hearing descriptions, in full detail, on what they had been through, we were not quite as gung ho, as before, for combat.

Fast forward to the 1980s. I'm in Ft Smith, Arkansas. I was working on *The Blue and the Grey*, the TV miniseries about the Civil War. One night after work my fellow actor, Warren Oates, and I went into town to try and watch a basketball game in a bar. The bar we chose had no TV. Three guys down the bar from us said they knew of a bar that had a TV, and they would be more than glad to take us there. I looked at Warren and he just lifted his glass of Jack Daniels, and he said, "No." Then he turned to me and said, "They said drinking was going to kill me." And it did a couple of years later.

I decided to go along with my new friends, without Warren. They drove around, and at some strip shopping mall, they got out to relieve themselves. Then all of a sudden we were surrounded by cops. My pals took off running. I heard a few shots, so I more or less just froze in the back seat. The cops yanked me out of the car and spread eagled me on the ground. They went through my wallet and saw my California driver's license. Not good.

One cop yells, "Looks like we got us one of them Hollywood queers, boys." The rest of the cops laughed. By now I was in handcuffs and a little more than pissed. I knew when they asked me what I was doing in Arkansas, I was in deep shit. I told them I was an actor and was working on a film here. This brought more laughter. This one fat cop knelt down, and grabbed me by the hair, screaming at me, "An actor, huh?" There was more laughter. The cop continued, "I supposed you're going to tell me you're Rock Hudson. You gonna tell me what you really do son, or you're going to get the worst ass kicking you've ever had." As soon as I said, "No, I'm not Rock Hudson, I'm Burt Reynolds," I knew I was in big trouble. That really pissed them off.

The next thing I know, I'm sitting in a jail in Ft. Smith. It's a tiny cell. One light bulb, which stayed on all the time. Ugly lime green walls. A day passed and still no one came for me. Nothing! No phone calls. Exasperated and scared, I knew I was in big trouble because I was supposed to be filming. That knowledge was worse than any guilt these scumbags could hand out. Another day passed, I think. I wasn't sure because when you don't see the outside and a light burns constantly you lose all sense of time. I sat down on my bunk. I ignored the fried baloney and gravy that was slipped through my food slot.

I heard a slight pecking sound coming from the wall to my rear. Someone was pecking out some kind of message, I assumed. Whether it was Morse Code or some jailhouse signals, I didn't know. I picked up a spoon and tapped back three times. The tapping from the other side ceased. I never heard any more secret messages from the other side. I'm not sure why my three taps ended the "conversation."

Now, when an actor goes missing on location there are only about three places to search; the morgue, the local hospital or the jail. Suddenly my cell door opened and I was ordered out. They took me to an office. I noticed the locals were now rather subdued. Some guy from the Governor's office and a couple of production people from the film company were there.

The Governor's man chewed out all their asses. Then he apologized to me and asked which ones I wanted fired. I looked at all of them, up and down. Finally, I said, "Nobody. Just make sure these assholes act a little more civil when they stop a guy from California." I left with the production people. As we drove to the location, I became very scared, knowing that I had probably cost the production a lot of money.

Andrew McLaglen was the director of this film. He stood about six foot six and was not anybody to trifle with. As I tried to slink back to my dressing room, I saw a few hundred extras standing at attention. McLaglen saw me trying to sneak into my dressing room. He grabbed a bullhorn and started, "Well people, I want you all to see John Wayne sneaking back to work. He then told me to get in my damn uniform." He continued, "Hurry, get your ass out here and you better know the *jokes*." He meant that I'd better know my lines.

Feeling very chastised and embarrassed, I came out of my dressing room, with as much dignity as I could muster. As I walked toward the set, I could feel all those eyes following me. The director seemed ten feet tall. I stopped in front of McLaglen, a very humble Yankee Colonel. Out of the side of me eye, I could see Warren Oates and Rip Torn cracking up. Stacy Keach tried to keep a straight face. An eternity seemed to pass. The director said nothing but turned around and said, "Action."

I sat in my chair beside Warren Oates, who could not resist saying to me, "You wanna know who won the ball game?" He was referring to the game we were watching when I took off with my local friends. I tried to ignore Warren's remark and eventually he gave up harassing me. Later, he told me, "Kid, just be glad you ain't working with Sam

Peckinpah." Warren shook my hand and said, "Don't worry about it. Shit happens." Nothing more was ever said about it again.

Later, I received a document from the Governor's office saying that I was now an official honorary Colonel in Arkansas. Again guilt by association.

I have even been put in jail accidentally. I was filming an episode of *The Incredible Hulk* in 1981. My character was a convict, with the words "Prisoner" printed on the back of my shirt. When I finished my scenes, I was in such a hurry to join my drinking buddies at the Universal Hilton that I never reported to wardrobe to turn in my costume. I drove out of the Universal gate still dressed in that shirt.

The Hilton was only a block away. But by the time I parked the car and started to walk toward the hotel, some cops had spotted me. Just like that, I was in handcuffs, being taken off to the Van Nuys jail. The cops checked out my story, and they let me go, with suitable admonishment. Once again, real life had intruded on my "make believe" world.

Charles Napier with friend, Buck McNeely on a huting trip in Mexico (1997).
From the author's collection.

Buck McNeely

In the entertainment business you meet all kinds of people: good, bad, friendly, nasty, etc. It's just like the real world. A few years ago I met one of the nicest people I ever met in the business. I was invited to a "celebrity shoot" in Nashville, hosted by singer Louise Mandrell. A "celebrity shoot" is a hunting event, but you don't hunt celebrities. Celebrities participate, along with "normal" people, and you hunt ducks, deer, moose etc. A charity will usually benefit from the hunt.

It was at a Nashville celebrity sporting clays shoot that I met Buck McNeely, who has become a lifelong friend. Buck is a skilled hunter, who works out of Cape Girardeau, Missouri. He has a syndicated TV show, called *The Outdoorsman with Buck McNeely*. The show started in 1985, and is now the largest syndicated outdoor adventure series in the US, broadcast on over 500 stations and several cable networks, both foreign and domestic.

The show is shot across the entire world, taking great video of hunting or fishing excursions. Buck could be in Russia, Mexico, Iceland, New Zealand, Africa, or the good old USA. Part of the appeal of the show is that Buck brings along celebrities. On various shows you might see Kurt Warner, Joe Penny, Dan Haggerty, Powers Boothe, Jesse Ventura, Frank Stallone, or me.

I went on a fishing trip with Buck in July 2000. We travelled to Lake Michigan. Little did I know that some of the best fishing in the whole world occurs in Lake Michigan. We chartered a boat out of Addison, Illinois, captained by Bob Jenkins.

The first day out on the water, I caught the largest fish I ever caught in my life, a 17 pound King Salmon. It took me awhile, but with the help of Buck and his young son, Max, I reeled the big king in. The Lake is an awesome body of water. Over the years the Fish and Game Departments of the states of Michigan, Indiana, Illinois and Wisconsin have developed a tremendous "put and take" program. They hatch millions of fish each year to introduce into the lake when they are the right size. These fish grow up to be caught and consumed by any angler that pursues these rugged game fish. Steelhead and King Salmon fillets are mighty tasty.

I remember one day when Buck's son Max caught a few fish, including the biggest fish he caught to date. We took turns catching fish as they hit the lures. We stood around the back of the boat *BSing*, relaxing for a few minutes and, soon enough, *BANG*, "FISH ON!" A rod would start bouncing, and one of us would yank it from its holder and hang on. The bigger fish would tear off on a run that stripped a half spool of line off the reel in a few seconds. That's when the real work began. That 15 to 20 lb. King may have 120 yards of line out, and he's angry. Using a pump and reel tactic, Buck showed me I had to horse that fish in three cranks at a time. By the time the Captain put the net under it and hoisted it over the transom, I realized what a powerful fish I had landed. My arms felt the strain, and I was ready for a drink. Proud? Yes I was. That was the biggest fish of my long life and I was thrilled. Max was also thrilled. I watched him tell Buck that this was the best day of his life. Buck replied that in a life filled with some pretty good days, this too was his best.

On another trip, Buck took me to Mexico in 1997 for a duck and dove hunt. This is where we really got to know each other. From the butt crack of dawn until we crashed at night, we were in each other's company. We stayed at a hotel in Los Mochis, Mexico. At 4am, a guide would come banging on the door way too loudly. We'd grab our guns and gear and roll into a van for a ride into the countryside. The van would pull up at the edge of a lake, and an airboat would be waiting for us. An airboat ride in the dark, before dawn, is quite an experience. They would crank that fan up and send us skidding across the water at 40 miles an hour. Flocks of waterfowl that roost upon the waters during the night would flush before the screaming airboat. Thousands of ducks, cormorants, curlews and many others migrate into this part of Western Mexico for the winter. Here they breed and fatten up on the abundant agriculture that has two growing seasons, before migrating north for the spring hatch.

The airboat would drop us off on a muddy spit of land, offload our gear, give us each a padded bucket and a case of shells, and then roar off into the darkness. We would lock and load our shotguns and wait for dawn. The marsh is a vibrant eco system. We'd hear flights of birds overhead before we could see them. I'd hear the whistle of wings and calls and feel the marsh awaken for a new day. As the light crept across the horizon, we'd see their silhouettes fly by. Buck would whisper, "Those are ducks, get ready." He then shouted, "Take em." We'd start blasting.

In the dark, I couldn't tell one species from another. Buck could tell if the bird was a cormorant, and then tell me not to shoot. I questioned, "Now how the hell can you tell that in the dark?" He answered, "It has a different silhouette from a duck or goose. See that long neck and those scrawny legs tucked behind it?" A few seconds later, Buck pointed to the sky, "Now look at that duck at 11 o'clock." I figured it out, but still wanted to empty my shotgun at everything that flew near.

For four days we got up predawn, and enjoyed several fine duck shoots. The action was steady and entertaining. At first I had some problems tracking those Blue Wing Teal. I kept shooting behind them. I worked to increase my lead and follow through, and started rolling them out consistently. I also make a great shot on a Pintail duck that was flying by. I led him for about a mile and the squeezed the trigger. "Head shot," Buck yelled. The bird was spiraling down like a helicopter, with his wings locked and extended. He hit the water, dead as a door nail.

One morning, a small boat with a couple of fishermen passed our blind. They started picking up our downed ducks. Buck said, "Charlie, they are stealing our ducks." Buck yelled at them, "Hey bandidos como sta? Pescador bandidos!" "What's that shit mean?" I asked. Buck laughed, "I called them bandit fishermen." I thought that was funny, so I started yelling at them too. We put up a pretty good heckle session but they never even looked at us. They scooped up as many ducks as they could find and went on their way. "I bet they need those ducks worse than we do," I mused. Buck replied that he didn't begrudge them. The ducks that we shot were donated to the local people anyway. They appreciated the fowl to add to their usual diet of corn and beans. After three to four hours, the airboat would come back to pick us up. They would net all the ducks we had shot and load them into the boat, and then they brought us back out. Lunch, then a siesta would re-energize our bodies for an afternoon dove hunt.

We'd drive into some rural village to hunt a local field or stand of fruit trees. Now these people were poor. I'm talking about grass thatched huts with dirt floors. The family would sleep in hammocks suspended above the dirt floor to keep above the night prowling varmints, insects and snakes. I did notice the kids were usually cheerful and quite clean. There was also a TV antennae sticking out of some pretty sorry looking huts, and even a few satellite dishes, which I got a chuckle out of. People will be entertained, no matter where they live.

One day we stood near a waterhole surrounded by an orchard. A couple of hours before dark, the dove would start coming to water before seeking their roosting trees, which was the orchard. After a few flurries, we noticed the dove was getting cautious. Instead of flying into the open area around the water hole, where we were shooting at them, they started flying the edges of the tree line, then ducking back into the trees. Buck and I got impatient and moved into the trees, and started ambushing the birds from cover.

The birds soon got wise, and sat down in the trees, waiting for dark and our departure. I remember Buck was angling around a tree for a shot, but stepped accidentally on a cactus. He let out a loud yell, and a few choice words, as he hopped on one leg, toward a log to sit on. I was laughing my ass off at him, as he picked out the thorns from his ankle. Buck cracked, "Good thing that wasn't a snake, or you would be sucking the poison out of me." I smiled and told him, "Naw, you'd probably die first if you were counting on that."

When you spend time with someone you click with, the bullshit flies fast and deep. And that is what kept us amused with each other. Buck asked me if I ever won any acting awards over the years. I replied, "Waiting for me to win an acting award is like leaving the porch light on for Jimmy Hoffa."

We had some great shoots. The ducking hunting was by far the best wing shooting I have ever experienced. Buck told me a few tales about Argentina wing shooting, where a man can shoot dove all day. I figured that would wear my old ass out in a hurry. I really did enjoy that Mexico trip as one of the highlights of my hunting career.

At night, we dined at the hotel restaurant. Being so near the ocean, we had an abundance of shrimp and lobster. They had a surf and turf special that included a steak, two lobsters and a pile of fist sized shrimp for $10.00. We ate like KINGS every night for *ten bucks each*. After dinner, we'd settled in at the bar and have a few drinks before we got wore out. Then we'd head for bed. One night, the manager put in a DVD of *Rambo II*. We watched it for a while. Buck said seeing me jabbering away in the dubbed Spanish was pretty comical.

I ran a tab at the bar and Buck mentioned that I had a $500 bar tab by the time we checked out. I guess I had a few Vodkas each night. He took care of it for me; what a pal. That's what good friends are for.

At the end of the hunt, Buck described me as a "world class wing shot." Coming from somebody with Buck's experience, that is high praise.

When you're on hunting or fishing trips like these, you really to get to know your fellow travelers. Because of the close quarters, you spend a lot of time talking with each other. That's why I feel I really know Buck. It's also why I feel he's someone I can trust, and whose friendship I value.

The Charles Napiers

In 1991, a musical group was formed in England. They called themselves "The Charles Napiers."

They took my name because they were fans of my movie career. They especially liked my role as Harry Sledge in Russ Meyer's *Supervixens*.

The Napiers were an instrumental group, playing a form of rock music with three guitarists and a drummer. They played together for 14 years, until 2005. They were moderately popular in England.

I never heard of them until 2001. I was able to get in touch with them, and sent them an autographed picture. I never did get to see them play.

But I was honored. After all, how many actors have a musical group named after them? You can still get their music on Amazon.com.

Dr. Phil

One afternoon several years ago (it's *always* several years ago), I came home to my ranch and family after a hard day in L.A. My wife, at the time, informed me that I was going to be mad because she had called the Dr. Phil show and had volunteered me to be a guest. I was rather stunned as I had no desire to be a guest on his show. She said the subject was to be about fame. I looked at her like she was crazy, knowing he would eat me alive. My ex said she was also going to be in the show. I asked her "Why?" I already knew the answer. Everybody wants to be on TV. So I gave in.

We arrived in Hollywood with two of my kids, Hunter and Meghan, in tow, and checked into the hotel. Right away I was pissed because they asked for my credit card. I've been through this game a million times. I asked the hotel if they had contacts with the show, and they said yes. I told them to call the show's production office and ask them to send someone down here, as I was not going to pay for the room. Shortly after, a couple of young girls showed up, along with a cameraman. I informed them that if they wanted me to be on the show in the morning they had to take care of the room. They acted shocked that it hadn't been taken care of. I told them that it was too late for them to book another guest, so either pay for the room now or I was going to leave. They did so, and my ex and two kids started up to our room. I found it strange that this little group from the show followed us.

Inside the room, I asked what the hell was going on. I didn't understand why was this guy filming me and my family already. They informed me this was standard procedure for all guests. I should have walked out then and there but I didn't know how disappointed my ex would be. Now this is where it gets interesting. They split up my ex and myself and started filming us separately. I went along with the game.

So here I am with this camera in my face and this young girl asking all sorts of intimate questions. (Here's the secret to his brilliance as far as I am concerned). As in most cases everybody wants to be on TV. And most people will do anything to get on the tube. I realized what was going on, so I decided to play along, although with a tongue and cheek attitude. They asked all kinds of personal questions, including whether I was ever involved in a homosexual relationship. I replied that it depended on what was at stake. Of course this didn't register with my intern, who was reading a list of questions given to her by someone on the show. Hence, that's the secret. If Dr. Phil knows all this beforehand, he would appear to be quite remarkable in delving into the depths of his guest (victim). I got bored with this and told them to get a limo and I would show them what fame was about.

They did so and we drove to Graumans Chinese Theatre, which was only a few blocks away on Hollywood Boulevard. Now, bear in mind that all this is being filmed, and certainly out of the protocol of the show. We pulled over to the curb in the limo. Of course, there were lots of people wandering around, looking at the footprints and signatures of famous stars etched in the concrete. Well, a limo pulling up finally got their attention. People come from all over the world to see this and NEVER see an actor. I got out, along with my entourage, and walked slowly toward the milling crowd. A couple of guys saw me and could not believe that they were actually seeing an actor. I asked them to play along and, unwittingly, they did. Soon the crowd sensed that "something" was happening, and they spotted me.

Now here is the point. Being surrounded by people looking for "something," I could have been anybody, but those two guys started yelling, "This is a *real actor.*" This caused me to have to dive back into the limo. Now mind you all this was on film, and I knew that Dr. Phil would look at this footage that night. I had no idea what his reaction would be.

The next morning, a limo took me and my family to Paramount studios. It always seems to come back to Paramount. I thought, "After all these years I come back to where I started: *Star Trek.*"

I won't bore you with getting settled down in the "Green Room." Then my ex and I were led to the stage. A live audience twisted and turned in confused expectations. Very shortly, Dr. Phil appeared to wild applause. I could tell he was pissed. His bald head was glowing red and I knew I had struck a nerve. The day before he had told the audience to stay tuned because tomorrow, he would be bringing one of his favorite actors on the show to talk about fame. Now, I was *not* one of his favorite actors.

I won't go into the interview. Let's just say, he edited the show to put me down, and at the end suggested I look for another line of work. I replied that perhaps I could become a greeter at Walmart. End of show. He left without even the slightest gesture of thanks.

When I told my agent to look out for a negative response from the show, the agent said, "Don't worry about it, nobody in this town watches that shit." So much for fame.

Agents

Some actors would say that agents are a necessary evil. I don't know about the evil part, but agents are necessary. Without them, you don't get work. And when they do get you work, they get a 10% commission from your hard-earned pay.

Somewhere in the 8000 or 9000 block of Sunset Boulevard is where most of the agents have their offices. For some unknown reason, the agents' offices are almost always on the 4th or 5th floor. Meyer Mishkin (mighty Meyer) was one of the best. Interesting, but no one before or since Meyer Mishkin had the foresight to put a talent agency together "corralling" all the mean or ugly guy actors, "the heavies." I'm told he started with Jeff Chandler, and then acquired Lee Marvin. The list quickly filled rapidly with Charlie Bronson, Claude Akins, James Coburn, Strother Martin, Luke Askew, Morgan Woodward, and Charles Napier (thanks to Meyer's junior assistant Don Gerler). If a producer wanted Lee Marvin, they had to take some other driftwood (some lesser known actor) along with the deal. Thus Meyer shrewdly moved each of us up the ladder.

When Lee Marvin was "hot" from *Cat Ballou*, producers couldn't get him. So the producer had to take a guy that was pretty much like Lee. James Coburn and Lee Van Cleef became stars this way. Meyer's waiting room was usually filled with bunches of these ill-tempered or ugly creatures (Bill McKinney from *Deliverance*, Robert Tessier from *The Longest Yard*) on any given week day.

All were in a foul mood, until their "turn came" to walk through that door and face the wrath of Meyer Mishkin. The periodic "ass chewings" were usually for some infraction or misdeed committed while "filming," maybe drunkenness or fighting.

I found myself squirming on the couch in Meyer's waiting room sometime in the 1970s, waiting for an ass chewing from Meyer. First in line was Lee Marvin. Sitting between Lee and I was the late, great Strother Martin, who was sobbing. Strother played many memorable roles in his career, including the mine boss in *Butch Cassidy and The Sundance Kid* and the warden in *Cool Hand Luke*. Strother Martin was the most sensitive and quirky human being I have ever known. But once you turned the camera on him, well, God himself would get blown off the screen. He was that great.

I quietly asked Strother, between racking sobs, what great "sin" had he committed? Lee Marvin gave him a withering glare, and then slowly stood up as his name was called. He sauntered into the lion's den as only Lee could saunter. As the door shut behind Lee, Strother really broke down into a huge, blubbering, funeral type of crying act. Between "sobs," he explained that he and Lee had just returned from a film in Mexico called *Joe Knox*. Later, the title to this film was changed to *The Great Scout and Cathouse Thursday*.

Strother scared the shit out of me again and sputtered that Lee and that "goddam Oliver Reed" had gotten into a drinking contest that lasted three days. Mercifully Lee had finally crashed to the floor

unconscious and the challenge was over. This contest had been hold-
ing up filming (not unusual in those times) and Strother whined that
he was being blamed for the incident and lost time. Lee suddenly
crashed out of Meyer's lair. He muttered, "See you guys across the
street at the Cock and Bull." And then he was gone.

Strother pulled himself into some semblance of dignity, as he received his summons. He took an eternity to get up, and then limped
lamely to his doom. The door slammed shut. We all listened intently
as even more horrible cries were heard, as Strother's confession was
indelicately extracted.

I don't remember much about my "lashes," as I was concerned
about the previous victims. After my session, I hurried across the
street and practically lunged toward the bar, only to discover Lee and
Strother laughing uncontrollably. Strother's laughter was more of a
hideous cackle than a laugh, really unnerving to say the least. Their session with Meyer was over and they were giddily happy. They were free.

There is another good story about Meyer and Lee Marvin. Lee
was a WWII Marine veteran. He was one tough infantryman, who
even got shot in the rear end on Iwo Jima. As is true of most foot
soldiers, he had no great love of officers. Meyer and Lee were flying
together to a film location. While waiting for the plane, Lee got hammered in the airport lounge.

Staggering toward the plane, he passed an Army General, also
heading for the plane. Lee reached up and swiped the General's hat.
He put the hat on his head, and boarded the plane. The General recognized Lee, and was too "star struck" to ask for the hat back. As luck
would have it, the General was seated near Lee and Meyer.

Much to the General's horror, Lee starts to gnaw at the hat. After a few chews, he puts the hat on his head. There is real tension on the plane now. The pressure was building. Finally, Lee dozes off. The General then makes a move to get the hat back. Meyer looks directly at the General, waiving his finger back and forth and mouthed the word, "No!" Meyer then gently eased the hat off of Lee's head, and he hands it back to the befuddled General. The other passengers burst out in applause. Meyer saves the day.

Meyer, as usual, had made his point and always had the last laugh. By God, we all toed the line. Meyer was one strong willed person, who could have a huge effect on an actor's life. He changed Charlie Bunchinsky's name to Charles Bronson. Meyer later told me Bunchinsky sounded "too communist." That was Meyer to a "T."

Fame

When you chose to be an entertainer as your profession, you realize (if you're realistic) that you will be a "has been" someday. Fame is fleeting. This fact hit me in the face a few years ago, when I attended an autograph show in Northern New Jersey. These shows usually invite various sports stars (past and present) along with people who have acted in movies and TV shows. Fans get an autograph for a price.

I was sitting at an autograph table with two men who were pretty famous in their day. Hugh O'Brian (of *Wyatt Earp* TV fame) was on my left, and to his left was Robert Vaughn (from *The Man from U.N.C.L.E.* TV show, *Bullet* and the great Western movie, *The Magnificent Seven*).

Traffic was not heavy, to say the least. When you're sitting there with several other "has-beens," the atmosphere can be very oppressive. Sitting to my right was a balding, middle age guy, with a long pig tail. He was drawing quite a crowd for his autograph, while the three of us were twiddling our thumbs. Hugh and Robert were quite dejected by the whole scene. As far as I was concerned, I was at least sitting close to the action.

During a break, I couldn't help but ask Mr. Pig Tail, "Who the hell are you?" He looked at me, smiled, and said, "I'm John Densmore. I was the drummer in The Doors, Jim Morrison's band." He continued to be busy the rest of the day. I guess that tells you that musicians have a much more loyal following than actors.

In the middle of the afternoon, with no fanfare, Hugh and Robert got up and left. I got a chill up my spine watching them leave: both of them big stars in the past, now reduced to the humiliation of total rejection.

As I watched Robert Vaughn pull away in an old Volvo with Connecticut license plates, I could not help but think, there goes the last member of the Magnificent Seven.

Some Thoughts on Acting

We all "act" in one way or another in our lives. When you tell a lie, are you not acting or just lying?

When you were a kid, you didn't really think about it when someone said, "Let's play Cowboys and Indians." You just did it. But today you are a mature adult and you don't do those things.

Actors show emotion like kids. Most adults are afraid to show emotion. As you get older, you have been trained not to show your feelings. But actors are trained to do just the opposite; that is, to *show* their feelings.

Lee Marvin and Robert Mitchum both had a very simple approach to acting. It could be summed as follows: "Don't get serious with this shit. Show up, know your lines and just do it." Mitchum, especially, was famous for his unique way of expressing himself about acting. He would say, "When I'm acting, I got three expressions: looking left, looking right, and looking straight ahead." Another time, Bob was quoted as saying, "I have two kinds of acting. One on a horse and one off a horse."

When I'm in a movie, I'm going to play "Charles Napier." Charles Napier is not just my name, it is a character I've developed over the years. I'm comfortable playing this character. Directors and producers know what they're going to get from me. That's why they hire me.

One time or another, stage fright happens to all actors, even the best ones. In almost forty years of film work I have very seldom been at ease in front of the camera. When I have been at ease, it has been a wonderful creative experience. Stage fright is nothing to be taken lightly. I have suffered my share of pain because of it. What makes this mental condition so terrifying? Logically it doesn't make sense. The worst thing that can happen is that you get fired. Getting fired from a film can have long term consequences, none of them good.

I recall a moment on the set of the sitcom, *Golden Girls*. Estelle Getty (the mother of Bea Arthur on the show) was standing next to me, waiting for a cue to go on. She suddenly turned to me and said, "I think sometimes I'd rather face a firing squad than go out there." With that, she made her entrance.

Robert Mitchum had a photographic memory. Give him a script. He read it once and he'd be able to repeat all of his lines. That's a wonderful gift to have but most actors have to memorize their lines the old fashioned way, reading them over and over. There are some techniques, or "tricks" actors will use to get around memorizing every line.

Marlon Brando was famous for having his lines written all over the set. They could be on any of the props such as a phone or a desk. What difference does it make, as long as the audience doesn't know you're doing it. I can remember a scene I was doing in *Rambo II*, where I had my lines written on a soda can. If it helps your performance, such tricks shouldn't be an issue.

I have been a "supporting" actor most of my acting life. That means I'm not the name above the title of the film; I'm not the star. In my role, I support the main stars. Your job is to add to their performance. You don't ever want to be in the position of taking away from the star's performance. A problem can arise if the star won't allow you to support or help him or her. That can make your job very difficult and seriously hurt your performance *and* the star's.

One important component of your performance is the director. A director is like the field general of an army. He's the boss on the set. An actor looks to the director for guidance as to how his character will be presented to the camera. Some directors can be very literal, requiring you to repeat each syllable or movement in the script. But there are some directors who treat the script as a sort of an outline. That director will decide how you say the lines or how you move around the set. They'll even change a line or two.

Jonathan Demme, a great Academy Award-winning director whom I have often worked with, did not worry about the actor repeating the script word for word. How the scene looked on screen was his ultimate goal. He would tell you that if you had an idea about your part or your lines, to let him know. He wanted to know your thoughts. That didn't mean he would accept your views, but he would at least consider them. What more could you ask for, as an actor.

Of course, you do run into a director who is incompetent. There are actors who think they can direct. And some can: Clint Eastwood comes to mind. But some can't. And Larry Hagman comes to mind here. In the 1980s there was no bigger TV show than *Dallas*. And, as J.R. Ewing, Larry was the biggest star on the show. Sometimes a star can wield incredible power on a show. Larry had the power. He wanted to direct, so the producers had to let him.

It was my misfortune to be cast as Bobby's pimp on the 1983 Dallas episode "A Ewing is a Ewing," to be directed by Larry. I was filmed for two days dressed like a pimp with flashy clothes and jewelry. On the third day I naturally show up with the same clothes, and Larry says to me, "Get rid of that shit." Since he was the director (and the star), wardrobe had to follow his orders and refit me with new clothes. Of course, all of the scenes I was in for two days had to be reshot, at considerable expense to the producers. Larry couldn't care less. One benefit of this fiasco was that I actually made more money, because of Larry's misguided "direction."

At my age, I can't physically do everything a director may ask of me. There is limit to the stunts I will do. Recently I played a sheriff in a low budget cowboy movie called *Shadowheart*. There was a scene where I ride my horse into an ambush. After all of these years, I can still ride a horse. That wasn't the issue. In this scene, I get shot. The young director wanted me to fall off my horse, after I get shot. I told him he would need a stunt double to do the fall. It's a long distance from the saddle to the hard ground. I wasn't about to break some of my bones for any movie, let alone a low budget one that would probably never see the light of day.

The director told me he couldn't afford a stunt man. I then informed him he had a problem. He solved it. When you see this movie (if you ever do), you will see one of the baddies aim his rifle at me, as I try to ride away from the ambush. The camera follows me for a while, and then shifts to the sky, as a shot is heard. Mission accomplished. The audience understands I've just been shot, and I didn't have to fall off the horse. Everybody is happy. A director has to realize the physical limitations of his actors.

Over the years in this profession, I have made and spent a lot of money. I have travelled all over the world. I got to meet some fascinating and very famous people. At times, I have had the opportunity to speak to students (mostly in drama classes), at various universities about my chosen profession. I let them know about my knowledge of acting, how films are made, how cameras work, and the insidious nature of this business.

To have any kind of success in entertainment, you have to want it badly and be willing to make sacrifices. I have made those sacrifices and they have adversely affected me in my relationships with family and friends.

After four decades, I find myself back where I started. Groveling again for another shot. Forget a break … just give me a turn at bat. It's crazy, but acting still brings life and meaning to a battered soul like me. Today I watch as my peers pathetically limp in for auditions. We've been competing with each other for all of these years. We've made millions. We've pissed away millions. Lots of women are entertaining men at houses we once owned. When do you pull the plug? *Why pull the plug?*

FINITE

Appendix

Charles Napier
Arranged by name of Film, Year of release and Role.

Films
The Hanging of Jake Ellis (1969) – Jake Ellis

Love and Kisses (1970)

Cherry, Harry & Raquel! (1970) – Harry

Beyond the Valley of the Dolls (1970) – Baxter Wolfe

The Seven Minutes (1971) – Officer Iverson

Moonfire (1973) – Robert W. Morgan

Supervixens (1975) – Harry Sledge

Last Embrace (1979) – Dave Quittle

The Blues Brothers (1980) – Tucker McElroy

Melvin and Howard (1980) – Ventura

Swing Shift (1984) – Moon Willis

Rambo: First Blood Part II (1985) – Marshall Murdock

Kidnapped (1986/I) – Lt. O'Bryan

Instant Justice (1986) – Maj. Davis

Something Wild (1986) – Irate Chef

Married to the Mob (1988) – Ray, Angela's Hairdresser

One Man Force (1989) – Dante

Hit List (1989) – Tom Mitchum

L'ultima partita (1990) – American Consul

Cop Target (1990) – John Granger
Sulle tracce del condor (1990)
Dragonfight (1990) – Moochow
Ernest Goes to Jail (1990) – Warden
Miami Blues (1990) – Sgt. Bill Henderson
Future Zone (1990) – Mickland
Maniac Cop 2 (1990) – Lew Brady
The Grifters (1990) – Gloucester Hebbing
Killer Instinct (1991) – John Doogan
Under Surveillance (1991)
The Silence of the Lambs (1991) – Lt. Boyle
Indio 2 – La rivolta (1991) – IMC President
Soldier's Fortune (1991) – Col. Bob
Lonely Hearts (1991) – Robby Ross
Frogtown II (1992) – Captain Delano
Treacherous Crossing (1992) (TV)
Center of the Web (1992) – Agent Williams
Hornsby e Rodriguez (1992) – Brian Hornsby
Eyes of the Beholder (1992) – Det. Wilson
Skeeter (1993) – Ernie Buckle
Loaded Weapon (1993) – Interrogator
Philadelphia (1993) – Judge Garnett
Silent Fury (1994)
Body Shot (1994) – Leon
To Die, to Sleep (1994) – Father
Raw Justice (1994) – Mayor David Stiles
Savage Land (1994) – Cole
Felony (1994) – Detective Duke
Fatal Choice (1995) (TV) – Nolan Global
Ripper Man (1995) – Harry
3 Ninjas Knuckle Up (1995) – Jack Harding
Jury Duty (1995) – Jed
Hard Justice (1995) (V) – Warden Pike
Ballistic (1995) – Underwood
Alien Species (1996/I) – Sheriff Nate Bridges

Spycraft: The Great Game (1996) – (VG) Frank Milkovsky

Billy Lone Bear (1996)

Expert Witness (1996) – Bonn

Original Gangstas (1996) – Mayor

The Cable Guy (1996) – Arresting Officer

No Small Wars (1997)

Riot (1997) – Agent Devaney

Austin Powers: International Man of Mystery (1997) – Commander Gilmour

Steel (1997) – Col. David

Centurion Force (1998)

Austin Powers: The Spy Who Shagged Me (1999) – General Hawk

Pirates of the Plain (1999) – Grandpa

The Big Tease (1999) – Senator Warren Crockett

Never Look Back (2000)

Down 'n Dirty (2000) – Captain Jerry Teller

Extreme Honor (2001) – Commander

Dinocroc (2004) – Sheriff Harper

The Manchurian Candidate (2004) – General Sloan

Lords of Dogtown (2005) – Nudie

Suits on the Loose (2005) – General Wilkins

Annapolis (2006) – Supt. Carter

The River Bridge (2008) (V) – Chuck

Your Name Here (2008/I) – Chuck

One-Eyed Monster (2008) – Mohtz

Shadowheart (2009) (V) – Sheriff Sanders

The Goods: Live Hard, Sell Hard (2009) – Dick Lewiston

Television Appearances

Arranged by Name of Show, Episode Name, Date of First Showing and Role

Cold Case: (1 episode)
    Shore Leave (October 26, 2008) -   Hal Chaney

Curb Your Enthusiasm: (1 Episode)
    The Lefty Call (September 30, 2007) - Bert's Dad

Ned's Declassified School Survival Guide (1 episode)
> **Field Trips, Permission Slips, Signs and Weasels: Part One** (9 June 2007) - Seargent Guard

Monk (1 episode)
> **Mr. Monk Bumps His Head** (20 January 2006) - Sheriff Bates

CSI: Crime Scene Investigation (1 episode)
> **Still Life** (8 December 2005) - Warren Matthews

The Batman (1 episode)
> **The Laughing Cats** (19 November 2005) - Killgore Steed (voice)

SQUIDBILLIES (9 episodes)
> **This Show Is Called Squidbillies** (16 October 2005) - Sheriff (voice)
> **Take This Job and Love It** (23 October 2005) - Sheriff (voice)
> **School Days, Fool Days** (30 October 2005) - Sheriff (voice)
> **Chalky Trouble** (6 November 2005) - Sheriff (voice)
> **Family Trouble** (13 November 2005) - Sheriff (voice)
> **Office Politics Trouble** (20 November 2005) - Sheriff (voice)
> **Swayze Crazy** (8 October 2006) - Sheriff (voice)
> **The Tiniest Princess** (29 October 2006) - Sheriff (voice)
> **Survival of the Dumbest** (10 December 2006) - Sheriff (voice)

The 4400" (1 episode)
> **Wake-Up Call** (5 June 2005) - Reverend Josiah

Justice League (1 episode)
> **Fearful Symmetry** (4 September 2004) - General Hardcastle (voice)

Dr. Phil (1 episode)
> **Fifteen Minutes of Fame** (23 May 2003) - Himself

The Mummy: The Animated Series (1 episode)
> **Like Father, Like Son** (8 March 2003) - Jack O'Connell (voice)

Son of the Beach (1 episode)
> **Three Days of the Condom** (9 July 2002) - Charles Foster Brooks

The Legend of Tarzan (1 episode)

    Tarzan and the Poisoned River: Part 2 (11 September 2001) - Ian McTeague

The Practice (2 episodes)

    Awakenings (18 February 2001) - Judge Abraham Betts

    Gideon's Crossover (11 March 2001) - Judge Abraham Betts

Diagnosis Murder (2 episodes)

    Sins of the Father: Part 1 (2 February 2001) - Johnny McNamara

    Sins of the Father: Part 2 (9 February 2001) - Johnny McNamara

The Simpsons (4 episodes)

    Pokey Mom (14 January 2001) - Warden (voice)

    The Fat and the Furriest (30 November 2003) - Grant Conner (voice)

    The Wandering Juvie (28 March 2004) - Warden (voice)

    The Seven-Beer Snitch (3 April 2005) - Officer Krackney (voice)

Buzz Lightyear of Star Command (1 episode)

    Haunted Moon (10 November 2000) - Wild Bill Cooley (voice)

Roswell (1 episode)

    Summer of '47 (23 October 2000) - Hal Carver

God, the Devil and Bob (4 episodes)

    In the Beginning (9 March 2000) - *Actor* (voice)

    The Devil's Birthday (28 March 2000) - *Actor* (voice)

    Bob Gets Involved (15 June 2003) - *Actor* (voice)

    Bob's Father (15 June 2003) - *Actor* (voice)

Walker, Texas Ranger (1 episode)

    Fight or Die (20 November 1999) - Warden Kyle

Party of Five (1 episode)

    Here and Now (28 January 1998) - Video Guy

George & Leo (1 episode)

    The Housekeeper (10 November 1997) - Dutch

Men in Black: The Series (7 episodes)

    The Long Goodbye Syndrome (11 October 1997) - Zed (voice)

The Buzzard Syndrome (18 October 1997) - Zed (voice)
The Alpha Syndrome (1 November 1997) - Zed (voice)
The Undercover Syndrome (8 November 1997) - Zed (voice)
The Symbiote Syndrome (22 November 1997) - Zed (voice)
The Inanimate Syndrome (6 December 1997) - Zed (voice)
The Psychic Link Syndrome (13 December 1997) - Zed (voice)

Superman (3 episodes)
1. The Prometheon (12 September 1997) - General Hardcastle (voice)
2. Legacy: Part 1 (5 February 2000) - General Hardcastle (voice)
Legacy: Part 2 (12 February 2000) - General Hardcastle (voice)

The Real Adventures of Jonny Quest (1 episode)
Without a Trace (30 December 1996) - Hinkle (voice)

Pacific Blue (1 episode)
Genuine Heroes (20 October 1996) - Tyrone Justice

Star Trek: Deep Space Nine (1 episode)
Little Green Men (13 November 1995) - General Denning

Hudson Street (1 episode)
Guess Who's Coming to Dinner? (7 November 1995) - Max Lester/Lone Star Sheriff

Lois & Clark: The New Adventures of Superman (1 episode)
Target: Jimmy Olsen (2 April 1995) - Salin' Whalen

Coach (1 episode)
Head Like a Wheel (17 May 1994) - Buzz Durkin

The Critic (23 episodes)
The Pilot (26 January 1994) - Duke Phillips (voice)
Marty's First Date (2 February 1994) - Duke Phillips (voice)
Dial 'M' for Mother (9 February 1994) - Duke Phillips (voice)
Miserable (16 February 1994) - Duke Phillips (voice)
A Little Deb Will Do You (23 February 1994) - Duke Phillips (voice)
Eyes on the Prize (2 March 1994) - Duke Phillips (voice)
Every Doris Has Her Day (1 June 1994) - Duke Phillips (voice)

Marathon Mensch (8 June 1994) - Duke Phillips (voice)

L.A. Jay (22 June 1994) - Duke Phillips (voice)

Dr. Jay (29 June 1994) - Duke Phillips (voice)

A Day at the Races and a Night at the Opera (6 July 1994) - Duke Phillips (voice)

Uneasy Rider (13 July 1994) - Duke Phillips (voice)

A Pig Boy and His Dog (20 July 1994) - Duke Phillips (voice)

Sherman, Woman and Child (5 March 1995) - Duke Phillips (voice)

Siskel & Ebert & Jay & Alice (12 March 1995) - Duke Phillips (voice)

Lady Hawke (19 March 1995) - Duke Phillips (voice)

A Song for Margo (26 March 1995) - Duke Phillips (voice)

From Chunk to Hunk (2 April 1995) - Duke Phillips (voice)

All the Duke's Men (23 April 1995) - Duke Phillips (voice)

Sherman of Arabia (30 April 1995) - Duke Phillips (voice)

Frankie and Ellie Get Lost (7 May 1995) - Duke Phillips (voice)

Dukerella (14 May 1995) - Duke Phillips (voice)

I Can't Believe It's a Clip Show (21 May 1995) - Duke Phillips (voice)

Renegade (3 episodes)

Fighting Cage: Part 1 (10 May 1993) - Brackett

Fighting Cage: Part 2 (17 May 1993) - Brackett

Windy City Blues (15 November 1993) - Sgt. Douglas Raines

The Golden Palace (1 episode)

Camp Town Races Aren't Nearly as Much Fun as They Used to Be (4 December 1992) - Mr. Smith #1

L.A. Law (1 episode)

The Beverly Hills Hangers (14 March 1991) - Detective Norris

Paradise (1 episode)

A Gather of Guns (10 September 1989) - *Actor*

War and Remembrance (1 episode)

Part 9 (8 May 1989) - Lt. Gen. Walter Bedell Smith

Outlaws (11 episodes)

Outlaws (28 December 1986) - Wolfson 'Wolf' Lucas

Tintype (3 January 1987) - Wolfson Lucas
Primer (10 January 1987) - Wolfson Lucas
Orleans (17 January 1987) - Wolfson Lucas
Hymn (31 January 1987) - Wolfson Lucas
Madril (7 February 1987) - Wolfson Lucas
Potboiler (28 February 1987) - Wolfson Lucas
Pursued (7 March 1987) - Wolfson Lucas
Independents (21 March 1987) - Wolfson Lucas
Hardcase (28 March 1987) - Wolfson Lucas
Jackpot (4 April 1987) - Wolfson Lucas

Murder, She Wrote (3 episodes)
Death Stalks the Big Top: Part 1 (28 September 1986) - Hank Sutter
Death Stalks the Big Top: Part 2 (5 October 1986) - Hank Sutter
The Dream Team (19 March 1995) - Denver Martin

Street Hawk (1 episode)
Hot Target (1 March 1985) - John Slade

Whiz Kids (1 episode)
May I Take Your Order Please? (2 June 1984) - Douglas Blackthorne

Night Court (1 episode)
Hi Honey, I'm Home (31 May 1984) - Mitch Bowers

The A-Team (2 episodes)
Labor Pains (8 November 1983) - Ray Cross
Fire (2 October 1984) - Army Col. Briggs

Gun Shy (1 episode)
Pardon Me Boy, Is That the Quake City Choo Choo? (22 March 1983) - Carlton

Tales of the Gold Monkey (1 episode)
High Stakes Lady (26 January 1983) - Tex

CHiPs (1 episode)
Something Special (21 November 1982) - Klane

Simon & Simon (1 episode)
>   **Mike & Pat** (14 October 1982) - Gibson

Dallas (4 episodes)
>   **Where There's a Will...** (8 October 1982) - Carl Daggett
>   **Aftermath** (5 November 1982) – Carl Daggett
>   **A Ewing Is a Ewing** (28 January 1983) - Carl Daggett
>   **Crash of '83** (4 February 1983) - Carl Daggett

Seven Brides for Seven Brothers (1 episode)
>   **The Man in the White Hat** (22 September 1982) - Marshal

Private Benjamin (1 episode)
>   **Benjamin to the Rescue** (6 April 1981) - Trustmore

The Dukes of Hazzard (2 episodes)
>   **Bye, Bye, Boss** (13 March 1981) - Digger
>   **Targets: Daisy and Lulu** (18 November 1983) - Pete

Concrete Cowboys (1 episode)
>   **Episode #1.1** (7 February 1981) - Red Asher

Walking Tall (1 episode)
>   **The Protectors of the People** (24 January 1981) - Vernon Larkin

The Incredible Hulk (2 episodes)
>   **The Slam** (19 October 1979) - John Blake
>   **Triangle** (13 November 1981) - Bert

B.J. and the Bear (5 episodes)
>   **Snow White and the Seven Lady Truckers: Part 2** (6 October 1979) - Hammer
>   **Pogo Lil** (20 October 1979) - Hammer
>   **Gasohol** (24 November 1979) - Hammer
>   **Siege** (19 January 1980) - Hammer
>   **B.J. and the Seven Lady Truckers: Part 2** (13 January 1981) - Hammer

The Oregon Trail (2 episodes)
>   **Suffer the Children** (1 January 1977) - Luther Sprague
>   **The Race** (1 January 1977) - Luther Sprague

Delvecchio (1 episode)
　　Hot Spell (14 November 1976) - Alt

Baa Baa Black Sheep (3 episodes)
　　Flying Misfits: Part 1 (1 January 1976) - *Actor*
　　Flying Misfits: Part 2 (1 January 1976) - *Actor*
　　Best Three Out of Five (23 September 1976) - Major Red Buell

The Rockford Files (2 episodes)
　　1. Two Into 5.56 Won't Go (21 November 1975) - Sheriff Billy Webster
　　2. New Life, Old Dragons (25 February 1977) - Mitch Donner

The Rookies (1 episode)
　　The Torch Man (11 November 1975) - Phil

Baretta (1 episode)
　　Double Image (15 October 1975) - Whitey

The Streets of San Francisco (1 episode)
　　No Place to Hide (25 September 1975) - Norderman

Kojak (1 episode)
　　My Brother, My Enemy (21 September 1975) - Marty Vaughan

Starsky and Hutch (2 episodes)
　　Texas Longhorn (17 September 1975) - John Brown Harris
　　Satan's Witches (8 February 1978) - Sheriff Joe Tyce

Star Trek (1 episode)
　　The Way to Eden (21 February 1969) - Adam

Hogan's Heroes (1 episode)
　　The Missing Klink (4 January 1969) - *Actor* (uncredited)

Mission: Impossible (3 episodes)
　　The Play (8 December 1968) - First Guard (uncredited)
　　Run for the Money (11 December 1971) - Thug
　　Cocaine (21 October 1972) - Roland (uncredited)

Index

Breinigsville, PA USA
13 January 2011
253206BV00006B/19/P